EMBROIDERY with BEADS

ANGELA THOMPSON

Embroidery
With BEADS

LACIS   Berkeley, California, USA

Typeset by Keyspools Ltd
and printed in Great Britain by
Courier International Ltd
East Kilbride, Scotland

SUPPLIES
LACIS: 2982 Adeline Street, Berkeley, CA 94703
    Tambour embroidery needles and beading needles

This edition reprinted 1992
for the publisher

LACIS
3163 Adeline Street, Berkeley, CA 94703 USA

ISBN 0-916896-38-2

Contents

Acknowledgements

My grateful thanks to all who have lent or offered work to be photographed for the book – my friends; members of the Embroiderers' Guild; the Scottish Branches, Jane Dew and students; the Smocking Group of the Guild; members of the Women's Institute; Tess Hayes; South Notts College of Further Education; and my City and Guilds Students. My special thanks to Helen Archibald, Muriel Best, Nancy Evans, Jane Lemon, Julie M. Milne, Sue Rangeley, Jennifer Stuart, and Paula Stypulkowski. For making samples for the book, my thanks to my daughter Jane Davies, to Janet Peacey and to Sean Carroll.

For generous help in research and for allowing me to photograph or sketch beadwork, I am grateful to Jeremy Farrell, Keeper of Textiles at Nottingham Museum of Costume and Textiles; to Louise Hamer, Curator of the Embroiderers' Guild Collection; and to Santina Levey at the Victoria and Albert Museum; also to the Museum of Mankind, and the Ashmolean Museum. I should like to thank Joan Edwards for allowing me to quote from her book, *Bead Embroidery*, Henry Spooner for demonstrating the making of glass beads, Ells and Farrier for bead samples, and especially Daphne Troughton for lending me her tambour beading hooks. Finally, thanks to my son-in-law, Peter Davies, for taking photographs number 11, 28, 40, 54, 56, 66, 89, and 130; and to my son, Timothy Thompson, for taking photographs number 25, 38, 60, 70, and 132, and for his patience and advice on photography and on using a word-processor. Tony Mason took great care in enlarging my black and white photographs.

Angela Thompson, 1987.

Introduction

Beads may have altered in shape and size throughout the ages, their methods of manufacture may have changed, but for the vast majority of people they still hold a fascination. As a child I remember playing with a box of beads belonging to my grandmother. She would tip some into the box lid, and I would shake them gently to and fro, mesmerized.

To the embroiderer they are an added delight. Seldom completely out of fashion, bead embroidery has once again come into its own. The aim of this book is to help those embroiderers who are new to bead embroidery, and to suggest different ways of working beads to those with more experience.

It is intended to give practical help and to cover as many types and combinations of embroidered bead-work as possible. For those with a deeper interest in the history of beads or other aspects and working methods, many excellent books are available: *Bead Embroidery* by Joan Edwards, *Beadwork* by Anne E. Gill and *Introducing Beads* by Mary Seyd are especially recommended.

It has been said that the story of beads is the story of mankind. Long may it so remain.

Author's note

Although both metric and imperial measurements have been given throughout the text, bead sizes are in general stated in metric alone, since that is the way beads are usually measured and sold.

1 | *The origin of beads*

Beadwork has been used as ornamentation from prehistoric times to the present day and is found in one form or another in the majority of cultures.

Shells of all kinds and pebbles with holes formed as a result of erosion by water have fascinated mankind throughout the ages. There is a basic urge to explore the hole and then to pass a fibre or thread through it.

Shells or pebbles which are difficult to find gain a rarity value. Several can be threaded onto one string and worn both as ornamentation and as a symbol of possession. They could be exchanged for food or other objects. Beads have always had a dual role and are valued for their form and workmanship as well as for their intrinsic worth.

Precious beads were associated with magical properties. They were used as amulets to ward off evil spirits, to preserve the wearer from danger and to guard against illness. Well into the present century children wore coral necklaces, while copper bracelets are worn today for relief from rheumatism.

We do not know if the art of making beads developed in one place and spread outwards, or whether the spontaneous urge to thread objects and decorate the body was one which arose in different cultures and at different times around the world. The nature of the source material for making beads means that there are many similarities; only specific types of decoration and manufacture can give an indication of their origin.

Beads used as barter found their way along the trade routes of the world. Although small in size, they mark the explorations, the endeavours and the surprising tenacity of our forefathers.

Natural objects

Prehistoric man used the hollow tooth-shaped *dentalium* shell or the bones of small animals to thread as decoration. In some places there was an abundance of seeds and plant material.

1   Bead strings
From left to right Shell necklace; seed heads and tiny seed beads bought in an Oxfam shop; modern glazed clay and copper bead necklace, Liebermann pottery; small clay necklace and a rough-cut turquoise necklace from Peru; massed strings of tiny seed beads, mid-twentieth century; Egyptian incised clay beads, modern.

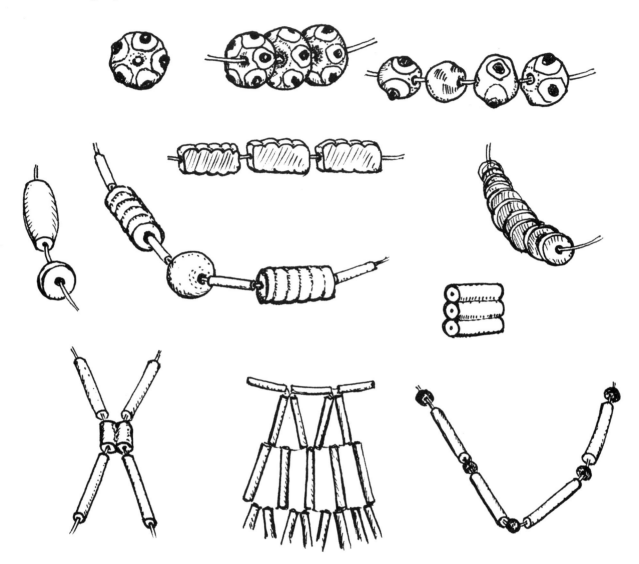

2   Egyptian beads, *c.* 1200 to 600 BC: glass eye beads, pottery beads, beads made from faience. (*Ashmolean Museum, Oxford*)

Seeds and fruit husks are used by ethnic societies, especially in the tropical regions. They are more varied and dry harder than those from temperate climes. Some are pierced while still soft, or boiled to soften before drilling.

The Karen women from the hill tribes of Thailand make beads from the shiny white seed called 'Job's tears'. They use them to decorate jackets worn after marriage. When the kernel is pulled from the outer seed, a small hole is left. They are dried in the embers of a fire to make them whiter. Originally a status symbol for the older woman, the seeds are used together with embroidery stitches to make various patterns.

It is difficult to follow the history of bead making in a chronological order as ideas developed in different places at different times. The great breakthrough was the invention of the bow-drill which enabled the worker to drill holes into the hardest of stones.

The Egyptians and the Assyrians were masters of this art. They worked carnelian, alabaster and even marble; but the turquoise was the most prized stone of the ancient world. It is found in desert areas as far apart as Persia, Central Asia, Mexico and South America. The first turquoise was mined in Malkat in Sinai. It was exported via Turkey, whence it derives its name.

3 *From left to right, front row:* bone whorl from Egypt, eighth to twelfth century AD; Peruvian clay whorl, probably pre-Colombian; clay whorl for spinning dog-hairs from Ecuador, AD 500 to 800; Islamic steatite whorl from Egypt, eighth to twelfth century AD; clay whorl for spinning dog-hairs from Ecuador, AD 500 to 800; bone whorl from Egypt, eighth to twelfth century AD.
Background: two Peruvian whorls on their original spindle sticks. Medieval period. (*Author's collection*)

Shells

The labour involved in drilling shells, which sometimes included grinding and shaping, was so great that shell beads were used as currency as well as for decoration and as a status symbol. In the Solomon Islands red shells were more valuable than white, red being the sacred colour.

Cowrie
Cowrie shells, which come from a hump-shelled marine snail found in the Indian Ocean, were highly prized as currency and can be found far from their place of origin. For hundreds of years they were exported from the Maldive Islands to India and even reached Siberia. In parts of Africa they were used as bride price, while warriors in East Africa wore them to decorate their quivers and war apparel. Even today they are combined with glass or plastic beads and sewn to a ground fabric.

Shells – North America
Between 900 and 1500 AD a cultural community in the Mississippi basin made large shell gorgets, disc-shaped chest ornaments engraved with mythical creatures. These were symbols of military prowess.
Wampum Indians from the north-east used cylindrical white and purple clam-shell beads called wampum. They were made from the inside of the New England *quahog* clam and took the place of earlier wooden beads. The beads were difficult to work and were highly prized. They were used as currency and to convey tribal messages. Belts decorated with wampum were worn at important ceremonies such as the signing of treaties. At first the clam-shell beads were manufactured by native artists, but later their machine production was taken over by the Europeans.

Pottery beads

Clay beads were at first unfired and disintegrated easily. With the invention of fired pottery they became more durable and were often decorated with incised lines and spots and, in later times, with additional colour.

Whatever the origin, there is great similarity between the different types of pottery bead. Sometimes it is difficult to tell the difference between pottery beads and the tiny clay spindle whorls used to spin fine threads such as cotton and linen. The spindle whorls tend to be less spherical, and more like a spinning-top. Two spindle whorls from pre-Colombian Peru in the author's collection, which were made for spinning dog-hairs, could easily be mistaken for beads. They are often sold as beads, and were probably worn as beads by later generations.

When higher firing temperatures became possible, porcelain beads were made from much finer clay and glazes were added to give colour and shine.

Precious metals

Superb golden jewellery was wrought in Ancient Greece and was exported to neighbouring countries. In Anatolia, the archaeologist Heinrich Schliemann made such wonderful discoveries that he thought he had found the necklaces and adornments of Helen of Troy. The Cretans were famous for the art of granulating gold, the method of soldering tiny globules of gold onto a metal surface. This technique spread to Greece and was used by the Romans. Then the art was lost and not rediscovered until the twentieth century.

The gold of the sub-American continent lured the Spaniards to exploration. Much beautiful work was lost as the gold was melted down and shipped to Spain. Silver is used in Mexico and in Asia and the Middle East.

Faience

Egyptian faience was made before glass was discovered, and was used to imitate turquoise beads. It was made by heating powdered quartz with lime and adding copper compound to produce a blue colour. Black and purple were obtained by the addition of manganese. These beads formed a large part of the wide, beaded collars worn by the Egyptian Pharaohs. When soda is added to faience and heated it turns into soda glass. Soda beads have been used in more recent times for bead curtains and for lace bobbin spangles.

Glass

Glass, made from a high temperature fusion of sand (silica) and an alkali such as soda or potash, is reputed to have been manufactured in northern Mesopotamia in about 3000 BC, long before the Egyptians did so around 1500 BC.

Eye beads

These were first made in Greece, near Athens about 2000 BC, as cult objects. They were later improved by the Phoenicians and have always been endowed with magical properties. In Turkey they are called 'Fatima's eyes'. Lace bobbin workers in nineteenth-century England called them 'Kitty Fisher's eyes' and considered that they brought luck to the lace pillow.

Alexander the Great set up a centre to establish a flourishing export trade in glass beads at Alexandria, while around 300 BC millefiori beads were made at Sidon. Later perfected by the Venetians, this type of work is still popular in the decoration of paperweights.

In Africa glass beads were called 'aggrey' beads and were traded at first by the Arabs. Later, Portuguese traders along the west coast of Africa bartered glass beads in their thousands of tons for slaves and ivory.

Venetian glass

By the eleventh century there was a thriving glass industry in Venice. Old techniques were copied, including that of making millefiori glass beads. The Venetians guarded the secrets of their glassmaking on the island of Murano, threatening with death any glassworker who 'defected' to another country. Those who escaped helped establish industries in Gablonz, Bohemia and in London. Later the Dutch set up their own glass furnaces for the production of barter beads near Amsterdam.

Trade beads

The tiny glass beads known as trade beads had an amazing influence both on the course of history and on the craftwork of ethnic communities worldwide.

The Indians of South America thought the green glass beads were jasper and traded them for gold, while the North American Indians almost abandoned their moose hair and porcupine quill embroidery in their favour. No European explorer ventured into the interior of Africa without sackfuls of barter beads. Woe betide the unwise man who chose the wrong colour or size!

Joan Edwards, in her book *Bead Embroidery*, has researched the records of HM Customs and Excise from before 1300. She tells us that the small beads known as 'bugles' were not necessarily cylindrical, as we know them today; rather this was a name for trade beads, to differentiate them from embroidery beads.

Beadwork around the world

Zulu beads

Before the advent of trade beads, the Zulu people made beads from seashells, ostrich shells and the enormous variety of seeds and dried vegetable peels. The wide assortment of glass beads enabled the craftsman to make new and intricate patterns with the bright colours.

Young Zulu children wear beads before they are clothed. Ceremonies at puberty and marriage demand the wearing of different beaded decorations such as collars and beaded veils. The marriage apron, made of leather, is sewn with an intricate pattern of beads while a maternity apron, made from skin from a buck killed by the husband, also decorated with sewn beads, gives strength to the unborn child.

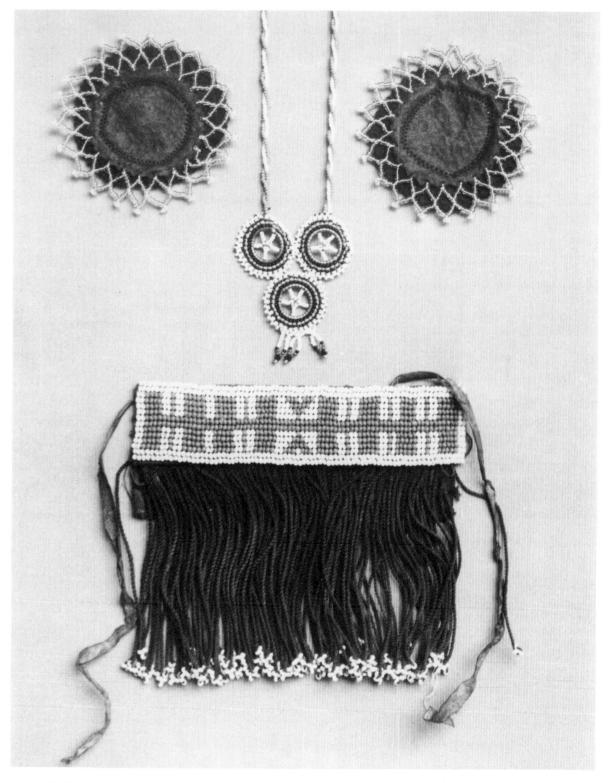

4   *Top* Zulu necklace and beaded mats made for the tourist trade, South Africa; *bottom* Zulu beaded apron made for tribal use. (*Author's collection*)

Beadwork was especially important in the conveying of messages. The Swazi and Zulu beaded 'love-letters' convey romantic meanings by the proportions of different coloured beads used, not by the pattern. The message is read from outside inwards, ignoring the borders.

The bead cult of the Yoruba

The Yoruba of western Nigeria and Benin produced a new art form, linked to a priest-king cult which they expressed in beaded crowns and decorations. Apart from cowrie shells, only a few beads had been available before the advent of trade beads. Materials tended to be used more than once; existing glass beads or glass bottles were melted down and poured into bead moulds.

Only the king wore the full complement of beaded artefacts which included conical head-dresses with beaded veils, flywhisks and ceremonial staffs. Priests were permitted to wear some solidly beaded materials. The beads became instruments of religious symbolism in ancestor worship.

The beadwork is all stitched, and features the 'lazy squaw' stitch or 'lazy-stitch' technique used by the American Indians, that of threading a group of beads before sewing down. Lines of beads are closely packed. Three-dimensional birds, completely bead covered, decorate the crowns as well as some of the panels and staffs.

North American Indian beads

Before the European settlers came, the Indians used beads of shell or clay. By AD 1800 Venetian glass trade beads began to replace the native beads. They were called 'pony' beads because of their method of transportation.

Beadweaving was worked on a bow-loom. Sashes and belts were sometimes made entirely of woven beads. Other weaving had the beads interwoven, strung and caught into the cloth at intervals, making geometric net patterns on the fabric surface.

Glass bead decoration, together with wool embroidery and brocading, took over from the moose hair, bird and porcupine quill work. Bead sewing methods were very similar to the moose hair and quill techniques, using the 'lazy squaw' stitch. This bead patterning decorated moccasins and other articles. It is interesting that moccasins with similar beadwork were worn by women in the plains of Siberia.

Short, close-beaded strings were worked over strips of paper to give a raised appearance to the beadwork. A different method was to thread the beads and hold down at intervals every two or three beads with a couching stitch, called overlaid, or spot stitch.

Design was much influenced by the convents and mission schools through the work of the Spanish and French Catholic nuns. European floral designs were often combined with traditional geometric patterns.

Some notable beads

Shishadur

In Western India and Pakistan the traditional 'mirror' embroidery of the desert regions evolved from the use of mica. Here talc crystals naturally separate into thin reflective sheets. Later, mirror glass was used, made from blown glass spheres, silvered inside and then broken into small pieces. Each region produced its own distinctive embroidery patterns. Some especially fine work was produced in Baluchistan.

5   Trade beads: Northern American Indian nineteenth-century purse. (*Museum of Costume and Textiles, Nottingham*)

6   Shisha glass with very fine buttonhole and chain stitching in brightly coloured threads. Cap from Baluchistan, north-west India. (*Author's collection*)

Today, coarse cotton cushion covers and other items are made especially for export. At Mariabad and Kalat in Baluchistan there are Government training and production centres where mirrorwork is taught to young girls.

The mirror pieces are held down with a network of buttonhole stitches. Technically they are neither beads nor sequins as they are not pierced; but their design use is similar and large sequins make an excellent substitute.

Iridescent beetles' wings

Beetles' wings were added to embroidery from the eighteenth century to the beginning of the twentieth century in India. In South India and the Deccan they were used on muslin. On cotton fabrics they were combined with metal thread and gold beads to decorate items such as hats and fans.

Tiny holes were pierced in the ends of the iridescent green wings to enable them to be stitched onto the fabric. In the late nineteenth century embroideries combining beetle wings with metal thread and floss silk were made in Goa for the European export market. Teacosies worked on a black ground were very popular.

Beetles' wings were even added to English embroidery of the mid-seventeenth century together with beads and spangles. In the nineteenth century beetle wings were used on both English and American embroidery and as decoration for fashion accessories and evening dresses up to the 1920s.

Pearls

Natural pearls are formed from a nacrous secretion around irritant grit or foreign bodies in both the sea-oyster and the fresh-water mussel shell. The latter are called seed pearls. Cultured pearls are made by the deliberate insertion of an irritant into the sea-oyster. These are examined at intervals and harvested when ready.

The seed pearls are found mainly in streams, rivers and lakes of the northern hemisphere. During the Middle Ages they were gathered in great quantities, and used to decorate religious vestments and holy books as well as court dress and royal regalia. Portraits of Elizabeth I show her great love of pearls which she added to her already lavish costume.

Joan Edwards, in her book *Bead Embroidery*, tells us that 'between 1761 and 1764 ten thousand pounds worth of pearls reached the London markets from Scotland alone'. They were much favoured in Russia where they were used to outline the figures on church embroidery and to surround icons. The Tsars made lavish use of pearls for their crowns and royal robes, while Russian peasant girls wore elaborate headdresses before marriage, covered with pearl loops and pearl embroidery.

In Lucknow during the nineteenth century, Indian rulers adopted the wearing of European-style crowns embroidered with glass beads, sequins and seed pearls. The pearl was pierced with the bow-drill. It was a delicate operation and wax was used to hold the pearl or a stack of pearls in position while drilling took place. They were sewn singly onto the cloth in conjunction with other gems and embroidery, or strung into a network and applied later.

Jet

Jet, which is a type of brown coal, comes from the fossilized wood of an ancient type of Monkey Puzzle tree which flourished in the Jurassic age, about 180 million years ago. Hard jet was formed by enormous pressure under the sea while soft jet was probably formed under fresh water. Hard jet is durable, while soft jet is more liable to crack and less easy to work.

Jet occurs in many parts of the world, but Whitby in Yorkshire is the best source of hard jet. It was discovered and worked by early man. The Romans prized the North Yorkshire jet and in the Middle Ages, rosaries were made for the monks in Whitby Abbey. It was not until about 1800, with the use of the precision lathe, that the Whitby jet industry thrived. The fashion for mourning jewellery in the Victorian era gave the industry a great impetus. So great was the demand that soft jet from France and Spain was imported and used mainly for the production of beads. Imitation jet was made from bog oak and from black glass, called French jet.

7 Jet and crystal beaded trimmings, late nineteenth to early twentieth centuries. (*Author's collection*)

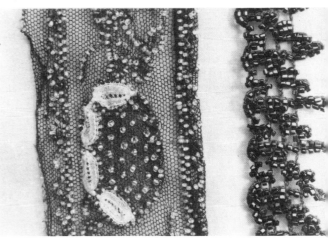

8 Beaded network collars: *top* African; *bottom* Mexican. (*Author's collection*)

Manmade imitations were made from vulcanite and Bakelite. Black glass, made by the addition of manganese during the melting process, was used mainly for jet beads and bugles for the embroidery trade.

Dresses, capes and fashion accessories were loaded with trimmings and fringes of jet beads. *Passementerie*, originally a trimming of gold or silver braid, was worked into different shapes and covered with jet by the tambour beading process. The sweated labour workshops employed women for a mere pittance in appalling conditions. A drop in demand, or a change in seasonal fashion, brought mass unemployment. After the First World War, the fashion for jet gradually declined.

Bead sewing and beaded network

There are only so many ways of sewing or stringing beads. One method may be common to several cultures. Beaded network can be sewn down or loose. The huge collars of the Eskimo women are made separately, as are bead collars from Mexico and, among others, the Zulu from Southern Africa. Geometric designs with each bead stitched to the cloth are common to both the African and South American continents.

2 | Embroidery and beads

We know that beads were used in medieval embroidery. Before this time the wearing of jewels, either hung around the neck, or as magnificent clasps and brooches to hold the cape or mantle, satisfied the decorative need. Jewel-studded armour was a sign of wealth and royal birth. The beadwork was at first confined to church embroidery, royal robes and regalia. A ninth-century convent-embroidered Hungarian coronation robe is said once to have been covered with precious stones and pearls.

The English word 'bead' comes from the Anglo-Saxon 'bede', meaning a prayer. This word was transferred to the rosaries which aided the counting of prayers. These beads were large enough to be passed through the fingers. Some were plain and simple, while others were of precious stone or were carved from wood or bone.

It was not until techniques for the manufacture of smaller beads and the drilling of holes in semi-precious stones were acquired that beads were more commonly combined with embroidery. Bead embroidery was worked together with metal threads for ecclesiastical vestments and church furnishings, often with the addition of coral, pearls and semi-precious stones. Opus anglicanum, famous for its underside couching stitch, featured beaded outlines to embroideries of religious figures. Many beaded outlines did not stand the test of time and existing examples show only the outline where the beads have been.

In twelfth-century Germany, vestment stoles of parchment were closely embroidered with seed pearls and beads, while the larger type of bead was sewn on vellum to decorate religious books of the thirteenth and fourteenth centuries. In Catholic countries, especially in South America, figures of the Virgin Mary and the saints are still clothed in beaded and costly jewelled dresses or loin-cloths. These are called 'image robes'.

The wearing of beads on clothing became fashionable in England in Tudor and Stuart times. Wealth was becoming more diversified and precious gems were sewn to garments for safety as well as for decoration. Very fine steel needles became available during the reign of Elizabeth I and enabled tiny beads and seed pearls to be sewn down. During the second quarter of the seventeenth century, small, square beadwork bags were embroidered with flower designs and simple all-over patterns, and presented as gifts.

Raised beadwork, often with the use of seed pearls, features on the Stuart stumpwork embroidery, originally known as 'stampwork'. On panels, beads were sewn individually, close packed with little sense of direction. They were also threaded on wire to form three-dimensional work on baskets, picture and mirror frames. Bead-sewn caskets and jewel boxes were embroidered by young girls. Some boxes were entirely bead-covered in a type of mosaic-work; others revealed little beadwork gardens within the lid.

During the eighteenth century the embroidered crewel bed-hangings had parts of the design picked out in beadwork. Hangings at Knebworth House had both the tree forms and the white background finely worked in beads. Contemporary French bookbinding also featured decoration entirely of white and coloured beads.

In her book *Bags and Purses*, Vanda Foster tells us of the mid-eighteenth-century French *sablé* beaded purses. The minute beads, as many as 1,000 to the square inch, were strung in correct pattern order, first laid across a framework then linked together by stitches (*sablé* means 'laid or covered with sand').

Late seventeenth- and early eighteenth-century court dress was elaborately embroidered. Gems and spangles were combined with fine silk and metal thread embroidery to decorate the bodice fronts and 'petticoats' worn by the ladies.

Joan Edwards in *The Bead Embroidered Dress*,

9 Layette basket, beads on wire, Stuart period, *c.* 1660–85. (*Museum of Costume and Textiles, Nottingham*)

one of her Small Books series, tells us that the French word *jais*, translated into the English 'jet', meant beads of many kinds and colours. Charles de Saint-Aubin, who designed embroideries for the French court, in his manual, *L'Art du Brodeur*, published in 1770, refers to bead embroidery as *la broderie en jais*.

Later, dresses became much plainer with the popularity of brocades and the new 'chintzes' imported from the Far East. The fine muslins and simple narrow dresses worn after the French Revolution and well into the first two decades of the nineteenth century were not so well suited for beaded embroidery. However, beadwork decorated the flat slippers worn at that time, and also the bags and reticules made necessary by the fashionable lack of dress pockets. Spangles, cut-steel paillettes and even feathers were added to embroidery, while beadwork tassels and looped fringes hung from the bases of the bags.

Pockets returned with the widening skirt, but smaller, knitted beaded purses remained popular well into the mid-nineteenth century. Beads were combined with the Berlin woolwork canvas embroidery which became so popular from the 1830s onwards. It was necessary that the beads should be regular in both shape and colour. The best glass beads came from France, adding lustre to the work.

According to Molly G. Proctor in her book *Victorian Canvas Work*, the beads were available in tiny glass bottles or small boxes at haberdashers and Berlin wool repositories. A similar box of French origin, containing tiny bottles of beads, is in the Embroiderers' Guild Collection. However, this box also contains strands of dyed horsehair and the beads may have been intended for a different purpose.

Fine- and medium-sized beads were used for the canvas work. They were sold by weight and thus were called 'pound' beads. Coloured glass beads were favoured by American women who finished off their work with tassels, fringes, ribbons and cords.

During the mid-nineteenth century, beads were added to a proliferation of items including scripture mottoes, cards, pincushions, needlecases, mats and doilies, chairbacks and even candlesticks. It was fashionable to wear bead-embroidered garments from the 1850s onwards. At first the beads were all sewn on by hand. In the 1890s an attempt was made to perfect a reliable bead sewing machine; but the bead sizes and shapes were too irregular. Eventually linear patterns using beads, which had first been

10 (*top*) Mid-Victorian beadwork pincushion with fes-
tooned edging. (*Author's collecion*)

11 'Grisaille' canvas embroidery: oblong stool top
beaded in shades of grey with tent-stitch background in
red wool, now faded; *c.* 1850. (*Author's collection*)

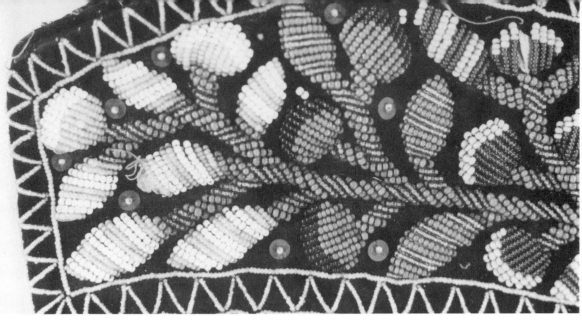

12 Glengarry cap, North America, 1870s: raised padding covered with strings of beads, additional seed beads and sequins. (*Museum of Costume and Textiles, Nottingham*)

wound onto bobbins, were sewn using the Cornely machine.

It is not known who first thought of using the tambour hook to attach beads. Joan Edwards, in her book *Bead Embroidery*, tells us that this method was first practised near Luxeuil, in north-eastern France, where they had already had success with the use of the Cornely machine. Much of the work was passed to outworkers who beaded *passementerie* and trimmings in their own homes. They were paid a mere pittance for their labour. Conditions in the sweated workshops were even worse. Queen Victoria had popularized the use of jet as suitable decoration for mourning wear, and dresses, capes and mantles were heavy with the beads. Edwardian gowns were elaborately beaded; but the fashion declined with the return to the narrower high-waisted line just before the First World War.

Surprisingly, it was the emancipated, tube-shaped dresses of the 1920s that gave rise to a golden age of beadwork. The heavy beads were tamboured or hand sewn onto light, flimsy fabrics, such as silk and georgette. Sadly, many of these beautiful dresses have now disintegrated under the weight of beads and fringing.

Sara Bowman, in her book *A Fashion for Extravagance*, gives a fascinating insight into this era. She tells us how the exotic Fortunay pleated dresses were weighted with tiny Venetian glass beads, painted by hand.

In the 1930s beading was worked on areas such as the collar, revers, shoulders and hip yoke, for daytime wear. Apart from a lull during the Second World War, the fashion for beading on evening dress continued. Elaborate work was produced for the *haute couture* fashion houses. During the 1960s and '70s beading was used to decorate the shorter dresses of the period. Beadwork has always been popular for theatrical work, and for ceremonial and royal occasions.

Beads of all kinds, including 'found objects' such as beer-can pulls, bones and plastic rings, were used on experimental embroidery during the early 1970s. During the 1980s a renewed interest in tambour beading for the fashion industry has been fostered in colleges of textile design, while the perfection of machine-sewn beads and sequins has given an impetus to the manufacturer.

The recent popularity of American television soap operas has encouraged the wearing of these heavily beaded garments. During a recent visit to Los Angeles, the author explored the boutiques on Rodeo in Beverly Hills. Each was like an Aladdin's cave with rack upon rack of heavily beaded dresses, blouses and high-fashion leather garments. These were even worn in the daytime; but the colour and sparkle were in keeping with the current lifestyle, and did not seem out of place.

On an even more recent embroidery tour of South Western China, a surprise visit was made to a bead embroidery workshop in the suburbs of Guangzhou (Canton).

Here, on the top floor of the factory, young girls were bent over large embroidery frames on which the dress fabric was stretched. None dare spare the time even to look up. There was no tambour work; all beads and sequins were sewn on by hand. Sequins were picked up singly and beads were scooped onto the needle from cloth containers machined to give a hollow contour.

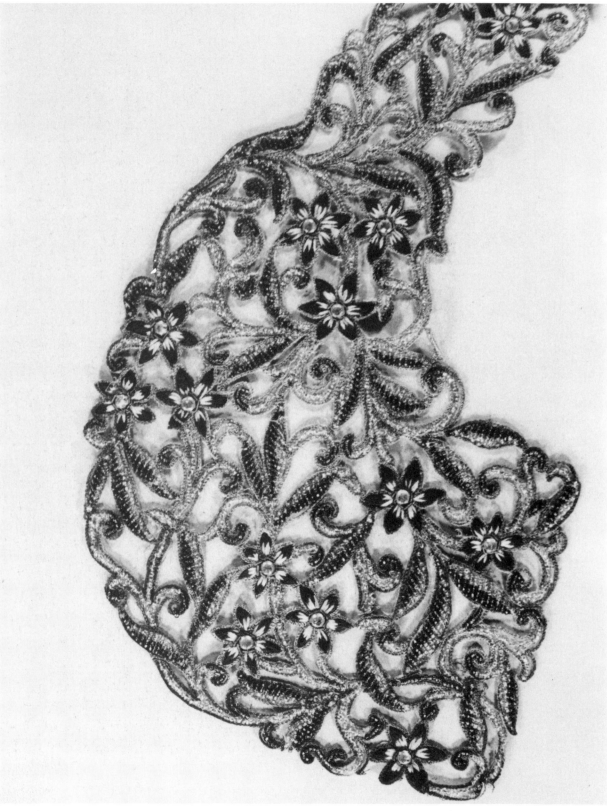

13   Bolero, 1890: tambour beading on muslin. (*Museum of Costume and Textiles, Nottingham*)

14 Dress panel 1910–20: mixed beading methods on voile and net. (*Museum of Costume and Textiles, Nottingham*)

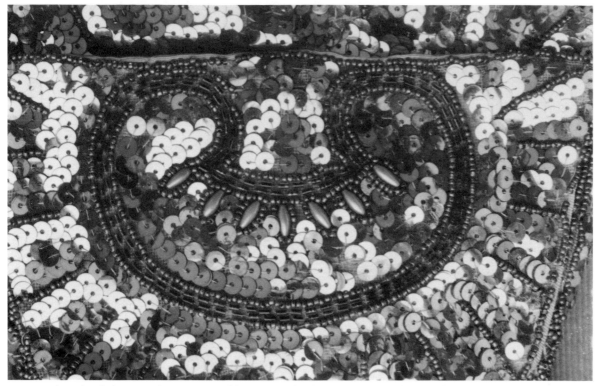

15   Tambour beaded evening bag, 1930s: golden sequins, bugles, rocaille and other beads. (*Author's collection*)

Later we saw the designs being transferred by rubbing a white paste through the serrated design lines. Other girls sewed up the garments by hand or machine. The dazzling finished products hung from the rails – the designs were the same as those seen in Beverly Hills. Here was the source.

3 | *How beads are made*

Sources and definitions

Stone beads

Before the invention of the bow-drill, shaped, soft stone and wooden beads or seeds were pierced with an awl, which was rotated between the palms of the hands.

The bow-drill, which had long been in use for firemaking, enabled the pre-dynastic Egyptians to become masters of the art of beadmaking. A sand- or grit-and-water paste gave bite to the stone-tipped shaft. An abrasive would convert the bow-string itself for use as a saw.

The earliest known drilled beads come from the Baderian graves in upper Egypt. Small pieces of the chosen bead stone were selected and chipped roughly into size and shape. The hole was drilled through the middle and the rough beads were rounded by rolling between flat pieces of abrasive stone. Another grinding method was to place the beads in grooves cut into gritty blocks of stone. For the final polish, a depression was cut into a wooden block and filled with sand and water, or sand and oil. The bead was pushed onto the end of the bow-drill, which was then rotated in the abrasive mixture.

Shell beads

Shells such as cowrie were drilled with the bow-drill and were then ready for threading. When the cowrie was to be sewn down to leather or cloth a hole was made at either end.

Large shells were broken into small pieces and roughly chipped into a circular shape. A hole was drilled in the middle and a series of these shell discs were threaded onto a thin stick. The cylinder of shells was then rolled backwards and forwards over an abrasive mixture on a stone until all were circular and the same size. This was an early form of mass-production.

Clay beads

Small portions of clay were moulded in the hand and probably pierced with a stick or piece of grass which would burn away in the firing. Later, clay was pressed into a variety of shaped moulds. As well as incised decoration, patterns were worked by scratching through a contrasting outer layer of coloured clay slip to reveal the body colour beneath.

The invention of mineral glazes gave brilliance to the beads. Nichrome wire, which does not crumble with the heat of the kiln, was threaded through the separated beads before they were fired.

Faience

Faience was made as a cheaper substitute for turquoise and is also called 'fake Malkat'. The mixture could be rolled out like dough, cut into shapes or pressed into moulds. There are some fascinating examples in the British Museum. It was probably regarded then as plastic is today.

Glass

There are two types of glass bead made by hand: those made from a hollow tube of blown glass, and the wound beads made from a heated glass rod. The latter was the method used by the Egyptians at Tel el Armarna under Akhenaten, father of Tutankhamun, about 1400 BC.

Wound beads
The making of wound beads was recently demonstrated to the author by Henry Spooner of Kenilworth, Warwickshire, who first made beads for his wife in the early 1970s for her lace bobbin spangles. At that time such handmade beads were virtually unobtainable. Mr Spooner perfected his methods after research into ancient beadmaking in the British Museum and at the Beck Collection in Cambridge.

Mr Spooner uses purchased glass rods between

16 Henry Spooner of Kenilworth making wound glass beads. The glass rod is melted in the flame and allowed to wind round the rotated metal rod.

1.2 and 1.5 metres (4 and 5 feet) in length. They come in a variety of colours, and white. A piece of rod is broken off, approximately 30 cm (12 in.) in length, and this is gently heated in a high-pressure gas flame.

In the past the beadmakers worked with oil lamps and it was only just possible with the use of bellows to raise the heat to the necessary temperature. Hence the term 'working at the lamp' or 'lamp-worker' to define a beadmaker. At one time there were over a thousand such workers in Venice. The fire hazard was so great that the glassworkers were banished to the island of Murano where the industry flourishes to the present day.

The bead is formed by letting molten glass wind round a heated metal rod or wire which is continuously rotated. The ancients used rods of bronze and examples have been found with the beads still *in situ*. At intervals the molten glass bead is 'marvered'. This term is given to the action of rolling the glass onto a flat metal surface in order to give it the required cylindrical shape. The glass is heated again and the process repeated. The word 'marver' is said to be a corruption of 'marble'. The Egyptians, who had no metal plates, ground two pieces of marble together in order to obtain a flat surface.

Decoration

The beads are decorated in a variety of ways. A thin glass rod, made by the heating and pulling process to the required diameter, is reheated and dripped into spots or wound in a wavy pattern onto the rotating molten bead. The bead is heated and marvered until the decoration becomes fused with the bead.

It is essential to cool the bead slowly, rotating all the time, or the glass will shatter. When cold the beads are removed from the rod by immersing in strong acid.

Millefiori glass

Millefiori decorations are still made in the traditional way from a series of coloured glass rods arranged standing upright into a chosen pattern, held together by a metal collar. When this is heated a blob of molten glass is attached and the whole drawn out to the required diameter. The principle is the same as that used in making sea-side rock, the pattern remaining unchanged when scaled down. The rod is chopped into small pieces when cold.

These pieces are used in the manufacture of millefiori beads. A plain, molten bead is pressed on four sides to flatten it and a piece of millefiori is picked up on each side. It is reheated and marvered until the millefiori decoration has become part of the bead.

Glass rods

Glass rods are drawn from the molten glass. The gaffer, who is head of his chair or team, takes a gather of molten glass onto his iron from the pot. He marvers it, reheats it and then swings it to an assistant who catches it on his iron. Two assistants then walk away from each other, drawing out the glass to the required diameter. The gaffer can judge the thickness by eye to the nearest millimetre. The rods are laid on a ladder-like structure to cool off. Today, these rods are made mechanically.

Pressed patterns are made by rolling the gather of glass onto a patterned marver. When the rod is drawn the pattern remains the same, but at a smaller scale. Single square-cut lace bobbin beads are pressed onto a pattern on all four sides.

Hollow tubing is made from a glass bubble blown by the gaffer which is then extended in a similar manner. Canes of fine tubing are cut into manageable lengths when cold, bundled and chopped into small pieces. These are inserted, together with sand and charcoal, into metal cylinders which are rotated

17 Adding the decorative spots in a contrasting colour with glass melted from a fine, drawn rod.

and heated to make the beads round.

Another method is to soften the chopped beads on a heated conveyor belt. This makes them more receptive for polishing when they reach the finely set grindstones. The chopping machines are set to produce beads of varying lengths.

Many beads are still produced, as they have been for centuries, in France, Italy, West Germany, Austria and Czechoslovakia. During the nineteenth century a small glass trade flourished in Birmingham, England. Today, seed and other beads are machine-moulded and made in India, Taiwan and Hong Kong.

Artificial pearls

Artificial pearls are made in different ways, but each method relies on the use of a 'pearl' paste. This can be made from ground-up mother-of-pearl or seed pearls, or from shiny fish-scales. One method, originally used over 300 years ago, was to coat the inside of a hollow glass bead with the pearl solution, or the bead itself was moulded from pearl paste and baked to set. Alternatively the bead was moulded from a chalk paste with applied leaf silver and varnish. Nowadays, embroidery beads and sequins are pearlised synthetically.

Crystals and jewels

Crystals or jewels may be mounted into a claw setting, or pierced by tiny holes at either end. Crystals are applied on their own or together with jewels, while jewels are more often mixed with beads and sequins.

Dr Marianne Stradal, in her small book *Needlecraft with Beads and Crystals*, tells us how the secrets of the art of staining and polishing glass stones were taken from Gablonz in Bohemia to Wattens in the Austrian Tyrol where the industry still flourishes. It was at Schumburg, which is near Gablonz, that the first glassworks were built in the early fifteenth century. During the sixteenth century the industry developed when glass-cutters and their families were attracted to the wooded area with its mountain streams.

Paillettes, sequins and spangles

A great deal of confusion lies in the naming of these tiny pierced metal or plastic discs. They have been sewn onto fabric, often together with beads and metal embroidery threads, for several hundred years.

Originally a paillette was a circular stamped metal disc, some 2 to 8 mm in diameter with a hole in the middle. A spangle was in use from Elizabethan times and is a small, flat metal paillette with a hole in the middle.

Any other stamped, metal shape, which had more than one hole, or one at either end, or with any number round the circumference, was called a sequin. Nowadays the word 'sequin' is in general use for any of these, and though not technically correct, has come into common usage. A sequin or paillette which is cup-shaped is called a 'couvette' or a 'cup sequin'.

Small metal spangles were added to embroidery or flat English quilting on Elizabethan costume. They were even more popular in conjunction with Jacobean bead embroidery or sewn at spaced intervals to the background of a panel or box-lid.

During the seventeenth and eighteenth centuries many fanciful shapes were stamped out and combined with metal threads for court embroidery. These were called 'paillettes percées'. Papillons were stamped from thin sheets of silver and could be colour-tinted to match the embroidery.

Spangles or sequins are combined with metal

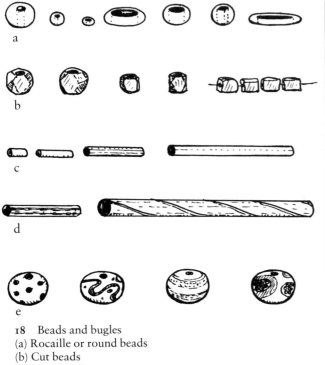

a

b

c

d

e

18 Beads and bugles
(a) Rocaille or round beads
(b) Cut beads
(c) Bugle beads
(d) Indian glass tubes
(e) Lamp beads

19 Small sample in a round, gilt frame showing different types of beads and sequins. (*Jane Dew*)

thread embroidery in India, Turkey and other western Asian countries. They add sparkle to an already rich embroidery.

Beads and sequins – types available today

Small glass beads

Small glass beads are made in different shapes, either round – rocailles – or long – bugles. They can be cut, faceted, coloured, lined or opaque. Their sizes and weights are referred to in metric measures. They are sold by the kilo, half-kilo or by grammes in specified amounts by the packet or in plastic tubes. For tambour beading they are sold ready strung. In catalogues the sizes are referred to by a number coding.

Round beads

(a) *Rocaille*   These beads are smooth inside and outside.
(b) *Tosca*   This a round bead which is smooth outside, but with a square-cut inside to catch the light. Toscas are also called 'square rocailles'.
(c) *Charlotte or three-cut bead*   This is cut three

ways on the outside (faceted). It can also be cut on the inside and metal lined.
(d) *Two-cut bead*   This is cut inside and outside and is squarish like a small bugle.
Beads with off-centre holes are used for alternate stringing or random effects.

Some beads are made in opaque colours or pearlized, while transparent or crystal beads can be lined with different colours. Others are silver- or gold-lined or have a metallic iris in a variety of colours. Some manufacturers make striped and rainbow-coloured beads.

Long beads – bugles

Bugles are like tiny glass tubes and vary in length from 2 to 35 mm. The outside of a bugle is smooth or ridged. The beads can be transparent, gold- or silver-lined, opaque-coloured or satin-finished. Liquid gold and silver-plated metal bugles come plain or twisted. Bugles are sold singly or threaded ready for tambour work.

Long Indian glass beads are available up to 50 mm in length, transparent with coloured stripes, or twisted and striped like barleysugar sticks.

Other types of bead

Many jewellery or threading beads are suitable for addition to bead embroidery. Very decorative ones are made in glass, clay, porcelain, wood, bone, ivory, and mother-of-pearl. Some are expensive, but could be used singly or for a special highlighting effect.

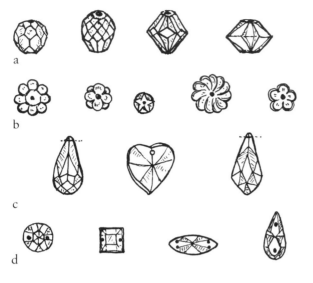

20   Crystals and gemstones
(a) Crystal beads
(b) Rosettes and marguerites
(c) Drops and pendants
(d) Embroidery stones

Metal jewellery beads

Round ones are available in gold and silver, 3- and 4-mm sizes.

Pearls and drops

Round beads, from 2 to 20 mm come in gold, silver, white or pearl colours. Pearl drops range in length from 10 to 20 mm (0.4 to 0.8 in.).

Plastic beads and pendants

These come in a range of transparent or opaque colours, including gold and silver, black and white.

Crystal cut-glass beads and pendants

Round beads and other circular shapes have a hole drilled through the middle. These include discs or rondels, marguerites (daisy shapes) and rosettes. Drops and pendants have a hole drilled across the top. Tubes are hollow, allowing the thread to pass through.

Crystals are available mounted in metal settings. The glass can be clear or iridescent crystal or tinted with a variety of colours.

21   Bead types: corner of a padded mirror frame using a variety of massed beads, bugles and sequins.
(*Constance E. Pepper*)

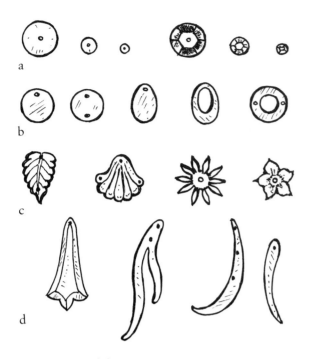

22   Sequins and shapes
(a) Flat sequins and couvettes
(b) Discs, ovals and rings
(c) Shell, leaf and flower shapes
(d) Pendant shapes

23   Repeat pattern for fashion embroidery using flower-shaped sequins and pearls. (*Jane Dew*)

Embroidery stones

Flat-backed faceted stones in a variety of colours have holes drilled at opposite edges. They are attached by glueing, pinning or sewing down.

Jewellery stones

Jewellery stones are made without holes, so it is necessary to have mounts if they are to be used for embroidery. In addition they can be supplied with special mounts for clamping onto the material with the aid of a clamping tool.

Jewellery findings

These are the small metal cups and caps, separating rings and decorative shapes that are used in the assembly of necklaces, and they may be added to bead embroidery.

Sequins

Although sequins are technically called paillettes, they will be referred to here as sequins in accordance with modern practice. They are machine-pressed from thin metal or plastic sheets.

Flat sequins

These centrally pierced discs range in size from 3 to 12 mm and come in a variety of metallic and pearlised or iridescent colours.

Cup sequins (couvettes)

The circular shape is stamped to form an indented cup with a small central hexagon surrounded by the six-faceted rim. Sizes range from 3 to 12 mm. The 5-mm (0.1-in.) size is used for tambour beading and the sequins are sold on a string by the thousand.

Shaped sequins

Many different shapes are made, some with a single hole at the top, others with two or more holes round the edge. There are leaf, heart, shell, star and flower shapes, discs, ovals, crescents, scimitars, diamonds and squares. They are made flat, indented or raised.

Sequin waste

The flat perforated sheets from which the sequins are cut are sold in rolled lengths. Small areas can be cut out and applied in conjunction with bead or metal thread embroidery.

Trimmings

A variety of already beaded pearl and sequin trimmings is available. They are incorporated with different embroidery techniques.

24 Pearl buttons embroidered onto the ear-flaps of a knitted cap from Peru. (*Author's collection*)

25   Small sample picture of rolled beads made from painted paper incorporating very fine metal cord. (*Muriel Best*)

Iron-on diamanté and pearl trimmings
The individual crystals and pearls come in two sizes. They are fixed to strips of paper and sold by the metre. The individual parts are cut and then placed onto the fabric in the required position before ironing.

Found objects

It became fashionable in the mid-1960s to include many different small objects in embroidery. Pieces of wood or even bones were applied to experimental embroidery.

It is possible to incorporate many objects which were originally manufactured for a different purpose. These include washers, rings, can-pulls, mechanical parts (from watches, etc.), buttons and fastenings, plastic bottle tops and caps, and other manufactured products.

Making your own beads

Many people prefer to make their own beads for use in larger-scale embroidery projects, while children find beadmaking both satisfying and fascinating. The following is a selection of some of the simple methods for making beads to be used for stringing or to give variety and individuality to applied beadwork for embroidery.

Modelled or moulded beads

Clay beads
A craft clay which sets without firing is a good modelling medium. The beads are formed by rolling clay between the hands. The round ball of clay is punctured with a metal skewer or knitting needle while still in the palm of the hand. Alternatively, model the bead around the skewer which is held in a vice or clamp, or stuck in a potato or lump of clay.

Pottery or clay beads need to be fired, either in a small kiln or in the hottest part of a domestic fire which is left to go cold before the beads are removed. If the equipment is available, glazes will add to the attraction of the finished product. (Children should only try this under the supervision of a teacher or competent adult.)

Press pottery and modelling clay into moulds, or roll into a sausage and chop into discs. The edges can be incised or serrated. Alternatively, the clay can be pressed onto a textured surface before cutting into shapes.

Dough beads
A stiff paste is made by adding just enough water to a mixture of one cupful of flour and two tablespoons of salt. The salt helps to stiffen the mixture, although too much will prevent the dough from drying.

The beads are moulded from the mixture and dried in a slow oven or over gentle heat. They can be decorated by the addition of powder paint to the dough mixture. Marbled beads are made by layering together different coloured doughs before the moulding or rolling and cutting process. A coat of varnish will add shine and help preserve the beads. Powder paint added to Marvin Medium (PVA) will make a colour varnish.

Rose-petal beads
These were popular in the Victorian and Edwardian periods. The author's grandmother used to make these and some very dark red ones were found in a small tin box.

Joan Edwards, in *Bead Embroidery*, explains that the method was to pick the dark, perfumed roses

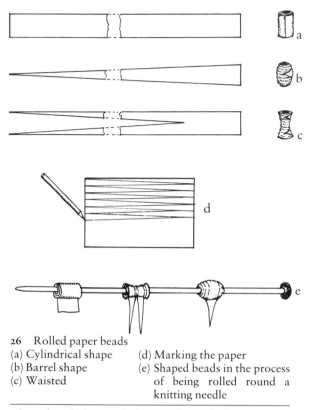

26 Rolled paper beads
(a) Cylindrical shape
(b) Barrel shape
(c) Waisted
(d) Marking the paper
(e) Shaped beads in the process of being rolled round a knitting needle

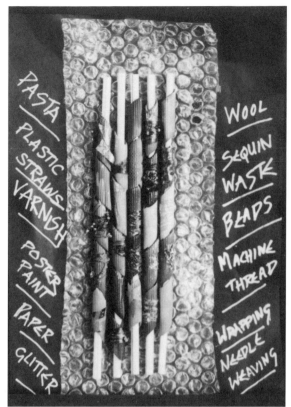

27 Pasta with straws, wrapping, corrugated card. (*Mave Buckroyd, City and Guilds Embroidery, South Notts College of Further Education*)

when dew-laden and chop and grind them. It was essential that the pulp should fall onto a baking tray made of sheet-iron and then set in a cool place for 24 hours. The grinding process was repeated on three consecutive days, by which time the pulp was ready to be rolled and moulded into beads. The beads shrink as they dry, and if left unvarnished should keep their perfume.

Paper beads

Papier mâché

This is made from pieces of torn newspaper or tissue paper. Use the softer type of newspaper, not the hard, shiny kind. Tissue paper is more expensive, but gives a finer texture. Soak the paper in warm water before tearing up. Squeeze out only the excess water before adding dry wallpaper paste to soak up the remaining moisture. Adjust the mixture by adding more paper or more paste until a suitable modelling medium is obtained.

Pierce the modelled beads and leave to dry. Smooth with sandpaper if necessary and the beads are then ready to be painted, varnished or sprayed with metallic colour.

Rolled paper

This is a very simple, cheap and effective way of making beads. Suitable papers are white typing paper, patterned paper or the colour-printed pages from magazines – the advertisements give a better colour range. Gummed strips of cut paper are rolled up around a knitting needle or skewer and left to dry before sliding off.

The shape of the bead is dictated by the way the paper strip is cut: the longer the strip, the fatter the bead. The width of the bead is determined by the greatest width of the paper strip. A width of 1 to 2.5 cm ($\frac{1}{2}$ to 1 in.) works best.

Start by using plain typing paper, making the strips the entire length of a piece of A4 paper. Mark out long triangular strips each with a base of 2 cm ($\frac{3}{4}$ in.). Alternate with bases and points at opposite ends to save paper. Cut out and spread with gum or paper-paste and roll up around the knitting needle starting with the base of the triangle. Little ridges will form as you roll, ending with the point. Make sure the point is well glued, or the bead will unroll.

It is possible to cut various patterns of strips (rectangular, pennant and spear-shaped) to varying widths. Leave the beads plain, or paint and varnish them afterwards. Coloured paper is most effective,

28 Front flap of an envelope bag (detail). Beading on a woven, pattern-textured fabric. (*Barbara Capewell, City and Guilds Embroidery*)

especially the shiny, printed kind.

Tubular beads

Plastic straws, plastic tubing
Tubular objects are cut to form a larger type of bugle bead. Plastic straws, either plain or colour striped, are chopped and incorporated into embroidery of a less permanent nature. It is possible to cut plastic tubing and coloured insulation sleeving with heavy-duty scissors. It is necessary to use a fine hacksaw to cut the outer tubes of worn-out ball-point pens.

Sticks
Any fine stick or dried grass that is tubular and hollow can be cut up to make beads. Bamboo has long been used in this way.

Wire
Wind a coil of fine wire round a fine-gauge steel knitting needle to form a small bead. The wire is wound back onto itself and cut close to the coil which is then slipped off the needle.

Drilled or pierced beads

Seed heads
There are many seed heads suitable for stringing. They should be pierced while still soft. Some, such as poppy heads, look attractive when spray-gilded after they have dried out.

Seeds
Nearly all seeds need to be pierced while still soft. The alternative method is to drill them when they are hard and dried or pierce with a red-hot needle. Some tend to split and can be softened by soaking in vegetable oil beforehand. A ratchet-drill is easier to use than a brace and bit. It is essential to hold the seed firmly by embedding it in plasticine or modelling clay.

In tropical countries certain seeds were boiled before piercing or drilling; but few of our European seeds are suitable for this process. It is possible to dye seeds such as melon and sunflower using cold-water dyes.

Dried vegetables
Slices of carrot or parsnip twist into convoluted shapes as they dry. Thread them together with seeds or couch down for embroidery.

Cut slices approximately the thickness of two coins and pierce them with a skewer. When a number of slices are threaded onto the skewer, leave in an airing cupboard or warm place until completely dried. The top slices, where the leaves grow from, are particularly attractive and look like fungi.

Stones or pebbles with holes in
A walk along the seashore, especially on a stony beach, will reveal many shells and pebbles with holes in, once the searcher has become accustomed to looking. Only the smaller and lighter ones should be chosen; the heavy ones are difficult to keep attached to a fabric background.

4 | *Bead embroidery techniques*

The methods of sewing beads onto fabric may be limited, but the possible permutations give endless scope to the bead embroiderer. We can learn much from a study of embroideries from the past – our ancestors were masters in the art of sewing on beads.

Tools for bead embroidery

Needles

Beading needles, also called 'straw' needles, are long and thin with a small, round eye. They bend easily and workers use this to advantage when scooping up the beads onto the needle.

Bead holes tend to vary in size. If the holes are very narrow and it is difficult to pass even a fine needle through when threaded, use a wire needle threader to draw the thread through. Workers in times past pushed a folded hair through the bead for the same purpose. If all else fails, unthread the needle and poke the thread itself through the bead. It is perfectly in order to use a shorter, thicker needle for beads with larger holes. Choose a round-eyed sharp, not an embroidery needle.

Threads

Traditionally, the thread was always waxed to make it stronger and pass through the bead more easily. This is especially important when using one of the modern synthetic threads which tend to fluff. Cotton is more likely to break, while silk is strong and pliable. Whichever thread you choose, it should be fine enough to pass through the selected beads.

Match the thread to the background colour, or to tone in with both beads and background. Sometimes a neutral-coloured thread is best. Transparent nylon thread blends in with both beads and background fabric, but is not easy to use. Alter the colour of transparent beads by sewing with different-colour threads. Experiment on small samples before the main embroidery is started.

Containers

Keep different types and colours of bead in little plastic tubes or small glass bottles. The cabinet sets with transparent drawers, sold to keep mechanical parts tidy, make excellent bead containers. The lids will prevent accidental spilling of the beads.

When working, tip the beads into a series of small plastic saucers from which they can be scooped onto the beading needle. Alternatively, cover the inside of a small box lid with dark-coloured felt and pick up the beads from this surface.

Backgrounds

In the past, beads have been sewn to materials ranging from heavy leather to the finest silk and georgette. It is possible to sew beads to plastic, paper and different weights of canvas.

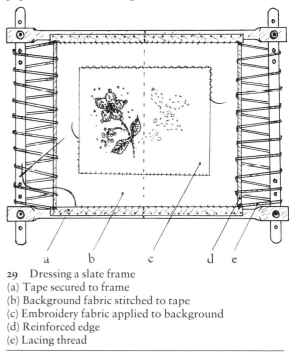

29 Dressing a slate frame
(a) Tape secured to frame
(b) Background fabric stitched to tape
(c) Embroidery fabric applied to background
(d) Reinforced edge
(e) Lacing thread

The chosen material should allow the needle to pass through and be strong enough to support the beads. A fine fabric will need backing. Transparent and semi-transparent fabrics are backed with net or a second layer of the original fabric; the two layers are treated as one. A backing fabric is not the same as a lining which is sewn on afterwards to cover the back of the work.

Do not mix fabric types. Back silk with silk, synthetic with synthetic lining, cotton with muslin, lawn, calico or mull. Support a very fine fabric with a firmer one. Thick ones need only a thin backing.

Framing

The fabric should be stretched in a frame of one kind or another. It is absolutely essential that the fabric should be taut during the working process. Beads cannot be sewn successfully otherwise. Tack fabric and backing together before framing the work, or frame the backing first and then apply the outer layer.

Tambour or ring frame

It is a great advantage to have both working hands free. A ring frame should be on a stand. The fabric is stretched over the inner ring with the hollow side underneath, keeping the grain as straight as possible. Push the outer ring over the top and tighten the screw.

Slate frame

A slate frame is made of four separate pieces. The top and bottom bars have a tape secured along each length. The background fabric is centred and sewn onto the tape, on the straight of the fabric grain. The side bars are either slotted into the top and bottom bars, or wind in the form of a large wooden screw. The background fabric is laced onto the side bars and pulled taut.

These frames are available with a stand, either at table or floor height. They are expensive, but well worth the investment.

Sewing beads and sequins to fabric

Stretch a piece of woven fabric in a small ring frame. Select different-sized round beads and sort them by colour or size into containers. Wax a 40-cm (15-in.) length of thread by drawing it through a piece of beeswax. Use a round-eyed needle which helps keep the thread in place. If the bead holes are large enough, knot the thread into the needle to prevent it from coming unthreaded.

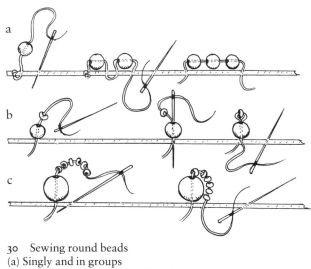

30   Sewing round beads
(a) Singly and in groups
(b) With an additional round bead
(c) With a string of small beads

Fastening on and off

To secure the thread firmly to the fabric, first make a knot at one end. Pass the needle from the front of the fabric to the back, with the knot on the top, and make two back stitches in the same place. The knot is either hidden beneath the first bead, or cut off afterwards.

To fasten off, two back stitches are worked in the same place. Run the thread between the fabric and backing, out to the front a short distance away and cut off. Fasten on and off firmly, or the beads will come undone.

Sewing round beads

With the thread attached to the cloth, scoop the needle into a saucer of beads until one bead slips on. This is easier than trying to pick up the beads individually. Slide the bead onto the thread. Judge the length of the bead and return the needle into the cloth so that the bead sits firmly in position. Too long a stitch and the bead will slide up and down, too short and the bead will not lie flat. Sew several more beads until you get the feel of it. Try different sizes. Every third bead, take a back stitch through the last bead. This is called a lock stitch. For greater security, make every other bead a lock stitch.

Little round flower clusters on Victorian beadwork were sewn in this way. The central bead is sewn on first and then five separate, surrounding beads. Any subsequent outer rings of beads are sewn down by threading two or three beads at a time, then taking a back stitch.

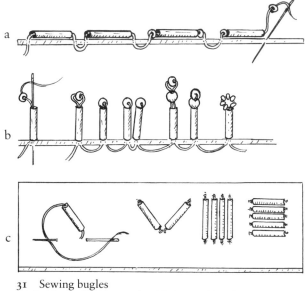

31 Sewing bugles
(a) Singly, laid flat or with added round beads
(b) Upright with one or more round beads
(c) Backstitched, zigzagged or in groups

32 Part-worked circular design using a variety of beads and close-stitched bugle beads. (*Constance E. Pepper, course work, Scottish Branches of the Embroiderers' Guild, Galashiels, 1986*)

Sewing with other beads

To sew a large bead with the addition of a smaller bead, first take the thread up through the fabric. With the needle, pick up a medium-sized round bead and slip this down the thread. Pick up a smaller bead, go back down through the large bead and the background fabric, ready to start the next one.

Sewing bugles

Sew on singly, taking a back stitch through the bead if the hole allows. Judge the length of the bead to make it lie correctly. Another method is to fasten on and then thread on a bugle bead. Insert the needle where you came out and take a stitch the length of the bead, twisting the thread beneath the needle as you come up. The direction in which the bugles lie will form part of the design. Flat-sewn bugles may be alternated with round beads or sequins.

Upright bugles

The bugle can be made to stand on end. The thread is taken up through the bugle, through a second small round bead, and back down through the bugle. They look best sewn in massed groups.

Stringing beads and sewing on

Thread several beads onto the needle before stitching down. It is like a beaded satin stitch. Known as lazy squaw stitch, this is the method used by the American Indians. The little strings of beads, from five to nine on each string, are packed close together in rows. Sometimes they were raised over a padding. This type of beadwork was a great favourite in Canada during the nineteenth century. A beadwork bag in the Nottingham Textiles Museum shows sections of little bead strings overlapping other bead strings. This opens up all kinds of ideas for modern interpretation.

Raised loops are made by sewing down the little string of beads shorter than its length. Too short a stitch will make the loop fall over; it needs to be just tight enough to stand up. Flower petals and leaf veins are sewn in this way. Shading is achieved by threading different-coloured beads onto one string.

Strings of tiny beads can be laid over a large decorative bead, or between the spaces of close-packed larger beads.

Couched strung beads

The method of couching is much used in ethnic beadwork. The North American Indians called it overlaid or spot stitch. All the Yoruba beadwork is worked in this manner. In the nineteenth and twentieth centuries some beaded purses were embroidered this way, while couched strings of threaded beads form the basis of the once-famous 'Berne' embroidery from Switzerland which featured on regional costume.

The beads are threaded, often in colour and

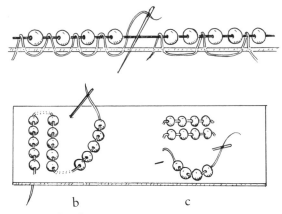

33 Strung beads
(a) Overlaid or spot stitch, couched singly or in groups
(b) Lazy squaw stitch
(c) Beaded satin stitch

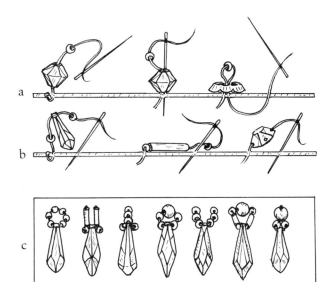

34 Sewing crystals
(a) Beads and marguerites sewn with an additional round bead
(b) Crystal drops, tubes and jewellery stones
(c) Attaching crystal drops

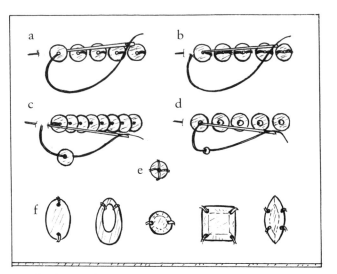

35 Sewing sequins
(a) Flat sequins sewn with a back stitch, stage one
(b) Back stitch, stage two
(c) Lapped sequins
(d) Sewn with a bead
(e) Stitched flat
(f) Sewing down shapes

couching stitch between each bead, using a separate thread.

Crystals

Heavy glass crystal beads are best sewn down with the addition of a small rocaille or round bead. This prevents the sewing thread from being cut by the glass bead and gives a neat appearance. Drops and pendants, which have the hole drilled across the top, should be sewn by threading first a small round bead, then the pendant bead and finally a second round bead before returning the needle to the cloth.

Any close-worked design can be drawn out on tissue paper, with the position of each bead or pendant clearly marked. This is tacked to the right side of the fabric, which should be backed and framed. The crystal beads are sewn through both tissue paper and fabric, following the pattern indicated. The tissue paper is torn away afterwards leaving the crystal beading intact.

Sequins

Sewn singly

Sequins with a central hole are sewn with a matching or contrasting thread, including fine gold or silver. Two, three or more stitches all come up the central hole and radiate to the outer edges.

pattern sequence, and laid across the working area with the thread ends held down. A second thread is used to couch between the line of beads, every two or three stitches. It is possible to build up very complicated patterns. Couching stitches need not be taken right through leather and thick fabrics, but sunk within the material.

In a second method the strung beads are pushed up separately and held down onto the cloth with a

Sewn with a small bead

The thread is taken up through the sequin and the small bead and back down through the sequin. Sew any combination of sequin and bead, or sequin, bugle and bead, or large and small sequin plus bead. These beaded sequins may be sewn separately or in continuous rows.

Sewn in rows from right to left

Single back stitch   Start by fastening on the thread and coming up through the central hole of the sequin. Take a back stitch down to the right of the sequin and come up again to the left, the correct distance apart to come up through the next sequin. They should just touch.

Back stitch   Secure the first sequin with a back stitch to the right. Come up to the left of the sequin and sew down into the central hole. Come up to the left ready to thread on the next sequin and sew in a simliar manner. There are two stitches in one hole and the sequins should just touch.

Overlapping sequins

Sew on the first sequin with a back stitch and thread on the next sequin. Make a back stitch to the left of the first sequin so that the second sequin overlaps the first and covers the central hole.

Shaped sequins

Those with several holes round the edge should be sewn with small, almost invisible stitches. Come up through the fabric and down into the hole. Embroidery jewels are sewn in a similar manner.

Sequin waste

Cut into strips or shapes and sew down with a toning thread at intervals, just enough to keep the shape firmly in position. Metallic thread will hold and decorate at the same time.

Sewing on findings and other objects

Small metal spacers made for necklaces can be sewn on upright, like cup sequins, or on their sides, using any available hole or space to pass the needle through.

A special clamping tool is needed for claw-set jewels unless they have perforations in the metal for sewing. Other large stones and objects which have no holes can be fixed by surrounding with button-hole or needleweaving stitches. This is the method used for holding down shisha glass or, as an alternative, large sequins.

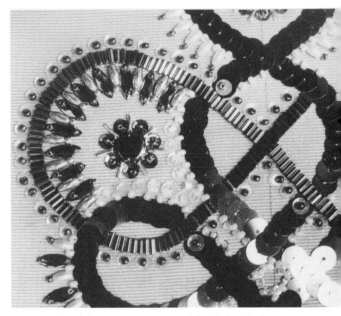

36   Interlaced design in sequins and bugle beads for an evening bag with handle. Part-worked motif showing stages in working sequence. (*Eileen Rumble, course work, Galashiels, 1986*)

37   'Fuchsia petals'. Detail of panel with applied fabrics and threads, french knots and a wide variety of sequins and small beads. (*Winifred Barry, Diploma Course, Mid-Warwickshire College, Leamington Spa*)

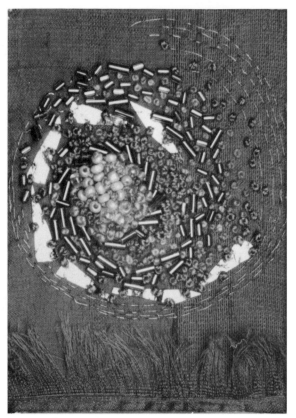

38   Small sample with a raised padded area covered with round beads, bugles and french knots with added silver kid. (*Muriel Best*)

Beadwork methods

Plan the beadwork as part of the initial design project. Beads added as an afterthought never look right. If beaded embroidery is intended to be heavy, don't be mean with the beads. However, adding extra beads does not necessarily improve a design.

When combining beads with embroidery, work the stitchery first and remember to leave room for the beads. First place any large, important bead and work outwards from this focal point. Stand back from the work from time to time to get an impression of the design as a whole, especially when working large areas.

Found objects are either best used sparingly or in massed groups of similar elements.

Canvas embroidery with applied beads

This method is not suitable for cushions or kneelers. Beads added to panels and three-dimensional work can give a lift to an embroidery worked only in wools, which absorb rather than reflect the light. In the design stage, areas of flat stitchery should be planned to make a suitable base for the beadwork. Small beads are sewn through both canvas and surface stitchery, using a fine, strong thread. Hold down larger beads with one strand of tapestry yarn.

Using massed beads as texture

The backgrounds of Stuart beadwork pictures and box-panels are crowded with tiny round beads, each one applied separately in a random fill or with beads strung and back-stitched at intervals.

Massed bugles were used as a fill-in. An altar frontal from Canterbury Cathedral crypt has a background of closely packed white bugle beads sewn in a series of wide waved bands to surround the canvas embroidered motifs. A similar white bugle background can be seen on an eighteenth-century piece in the Nottingham Museum of Textiles. A white bugle background surrounds metal thread and chenille embroidery on large panels in Hauteville House, Guernsey.

These close-sewn bugle beads give an extraordinary textural effect. This was sometimes achieved by first threading the bugle beads onto thin wire which was couched down between the beads. The slight stiffness of the wire helped to form the waved lines.

In the Embroiderers' Guild Collection, a trim from a French 1920s dress shows pink bugles applied to net by hand, filling spaces between raised metal thread embroidery motifs. The bugles are sewn in straight lines, the gaps alternating as on a brick wall.

The modern tendency is to pile up beads in crunchy areas of texture. Vary the type of bead to make contrasting smoother sections. Joyce Law has used this method to advantage on a shoulder decoration now in the Guild Collection (1983). Small areas are outlined with clasped crystal jewels and infilled with random bugles and mixtures of smaller beads.

Using beads spaced out

Single beads are sewn at intervals to make a grid or background pattern. A Stuart beadwork basket in the Nottingham Museum of Textiles has a background infill of spaced sequins attached by small beads. Linear designs of scattered beads need careful planning or they look spotty. Gradation of bead size as well as colour and type can alter the look of the work. Outline printed fabric designs with small beads or use them to texture already printed fabrics.

Beadwork on net, lace and fine fabrics

Let the sewing thread match the background colour on all transparent fabrics, whether they are mounted or not. Draw the design on paper, place beneath the frame and tack outlines through the fabric only.

Net

Beads are sewn onto fine net using a back stitch and are worked in continuous or linear designs in order to limit fastening on and off. The thread should be tied in position to begin, and tied off to finish. Beads should be large enough not to fall through the mesh.

Sew small beads along the gauge lines of large-patterned curtain net, or string the beads between the net openings. Large-scale vegetable or plastic netting makes a basis for experimental bead embroidery.

Lace

Beads are added to lace to border outlines, to centre a flower or to add highlights to certain areas. Combine sequins and small bugle beads for variety. Beaded lace edgings are best sewn with very fine beads.

Fine fabrics

Spaced beading, with the thread taken across the back of the work, may be sewn onto semi-opaque fabrics. Back stitching is used to hold the beads firmly in position. A net backing is essential for anything heavier than sequins. This includes large fish-scale paillettes which are hand sewn in rows across the fabric. Each row overlaps as in a pantiled roof with the long thread taken across the back. Sew sequins separately or string and couch them at intervals.

Silk is treated as any other fine fabric. Sharp-edged beads can catch on fine silk, so test them first by rubbing through the fingers. Add beads to the centres of silk flowers and any applied decoration.

A very delicate effect is achieved by sewing beads onto one layer of fine fabric and covering this with another layer. More beads can be applied on top. While working on pale fabrics it may be necessary to cover with tissue paper, tacked in place using a light-coloured thread.

Machine embroidery

The beadwork should follow the narrow lines of free embroidery as closely as possible, to become

39 'Woodland'. Machine embroidery with detached leaves and added beads. (*Sylvia Amner*)

part of it. Use beads in the centre of flowers or in other important parts of the design. Keep the beads small in scale, even when adding to wide satin stitch embroidery.

Sequins

Machine embroidery is worked after these are sewn to the fabric. Position the sequins, leaving enough space to machine around each one.

Whipped or feather stitch

Set the machine for free embroidery by dropping or covering the feed teeth and removing the foot. Sew the sequins in position. Place the fabric, right side on top, into the embroidery hoop with the hollow side uppermost. Thread the machine with a strong upper thread and a fine bobbin thread. Tighten the top tension and machine freely with a circular motion around each sequin. The bottom thread should pile up into tiny spiked circles.

Eyelets

Place sequins beneath machine-worked eyelets and sew them in position onto a backing fabric.

Machine texture

Beadwork may look too heavy when combined with

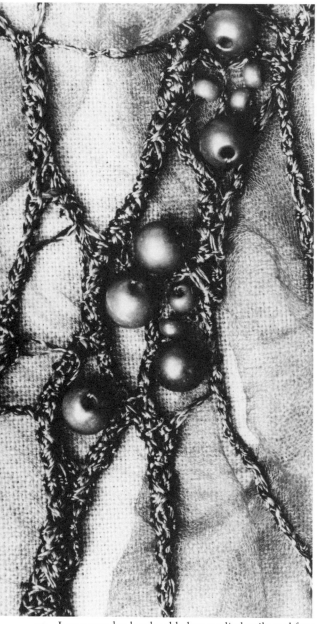

40   Large wooden beads added to applied voile and free needleweaving. Small sample to suggest scaly texture. (*Marie Roper, Dragon Project, Advanced City and Guilds Embroidery*)

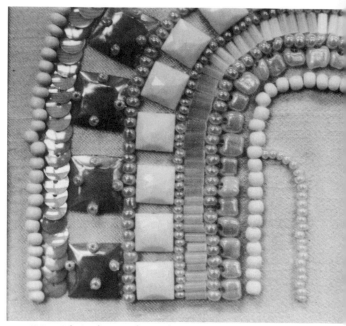

41   'Moorish Arches' with pearls, sequins and moulded plastic beads. Section of a panel, one of a series on the theme of architecture. (*Jane Dew*)

fine machine embroidery. Satin stitch will give a thicker line, or you can sew rows of loops using the tailor-tacking foot. This foot has a raised flange in the middle over which the loops are formed. It is normally used for marking pattern outlines with lines of spaced loops. By setting the machine to a short stitch length, close lines of decorative loops can be sewn. It looks attractive when worked in shaded thread. It is necessary to fix the loops with iron-on interfacing on the back of the work, so the beadwork should be added afterwards.

If you have access to a Cornely trade machine, work chain stitch or the loopy moss stitch in fine wools. Moss stitch is a part-worked chain stitch and will need securing from behind with iron-on interfacing before the beads are applied.

Design

Sources and ideas

Beadwork is formed of separate units. The beads and sequins have to be assembled in such a way that they integrate harmoniously. The simplest method is to add beads as part of an already created design, whether it is painted or printed on fabric, or part of an embroidery technique. This is effective, but not completely satisfying.

The problem can be approached from a different angle. Since bead embroidery is of necessity formed from many small parts, let the design source material start in a similar manner.

Any medium that has texture or broken lines, that is itself formed from small dots such as a blown-up newspaper print, makes a good starting

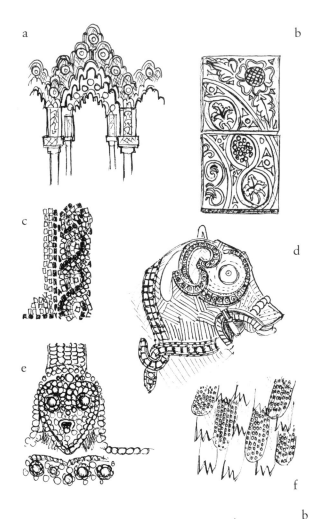

a

b

c

e

d

f

42 Design sources for beadwork
(a) Moorish architecture, the Alhambra Palace
(b) Medieval tiles, fourteenth century (British Museum)
(c) Romano-British mosaic pavement
(d) Viking gilt-bronze harness terminal (British Museum)
(e) Viking silver crucifix (British Museum)
(f) Magnified scales of a butterfly's wing

point. Others include textured rubbings, wood-block prints, nail pictures, raked lines on sand, photographs of cell structure, pebbles on a beach.

Other design sources can be found in nature drawings, architecture, black-and-white photographs, cut-up newsprint of differing density, magazines and books or computer graphics. Ideas can also be gleaned from the study of examples of historic beadwork, although design interpretations should reflect present-day thoughts rather than those of yesterday. Sketch the actual beadwork, the object being to study it closely. A photograph records the piece; drawing focuses the mind and aids the memory.

43 Stretching and mounting work
(a) Finished embroidery pinned out from the centre of each side onto a board covered with dampened blotting paper
(b) Back view – lacing the finished work over hardboard, starting from the centres
(c) Lacing the opposite way, catching in the folded, mitred corners

b

a

c

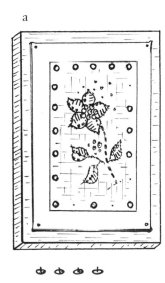

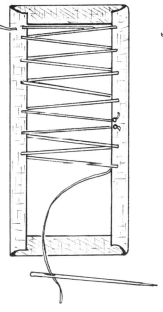

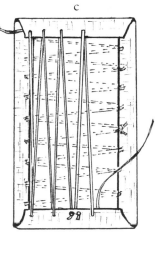

Translating design to beadwork

Black-and-white photographs or newspaper cuttings are easier to interpret than colour. It may be necessary to select only a part of a design source. Cut two L-shaped pieces of card and move across the print to make a variable window. The main design lines can then be drawn or traced off.

Enlarging

Increase the size of the chosen area, either by drawing by eye, or squaring off with a grid and translating to a larger-scale grid. The design may need to be simplified. A drawing could go through several stages before a satisfactory result is obtained. The design section can be mirror-imaged or used as a repeat.

It is worth taking trouble at this stage, as bead embroidery is a slow process and not conducive to alteration. Only when you are absolutely satisfied should you transfer the design to the fabric.

Transferring a design to the fabric

Do not use marking pens or rely on tailor's chalk. Trace your design onto tissue paper, pin this onto the fabric and tack along the design lines with tacking threads to match the background fabric. (It may not be possible to remove them all afterwards if they are caught in the bead embroidery.)

When all is tacked, slit along the design lines on the paper with the eye end of a needle, joining up the holes. This splits the paper along the lines and the paper can be lifted away without pulling the tacking thread. This is best done after the fabric has been framed.

Finishing

Stretching

Some embroidery, especially machine work, tends to draw up the fabric and it may need stretching. First test to make sure neither the fabric nor the beads mark when dampened. With the right side uppermost, pin out all four sides equally, starting from the centres, onto a board covered with layers of lightly dampened blotting paper. Do not wet the fabric. Remove when absolutely dry.

Mounting work

Bead embroidery for panels and box-lids should be strung and laced over card or hardboard, keeping the fabric grain straight. A layer of soft fabric or thin quilting wadding placed underneath will give a softer effect and allow the beadwork to lie even.

5 | *Beadwork for fashion, the theatre and the church*

Fashion

Sewn beadwork

The tradition of applying beaded decoration to costume goes back hundreds of years. At one time, wealth was worn on the person, the richness of the applied jewels and pearls proclaiming the wealth and status of the wearer.

Even today, bead decoration is expensive, especially if the beads are applied by hand stitchery. Many of the exclusive beaded and sequinned garments are worked with the tambour beading hook. Beadwork for mass-produced fashion is worked by machine.

A bead embroiderer who is also a dressmaker has an advantage here, being able to create individual garments where the greatest cost is in the labour of the actual beadwork.

Design and application

The choice of fabric determines the type of beading possible. Avoid heavy beading on lightweight fabrics. During the 1920s very heavy beads were worked onto fine fabrics. The purpose of this was to make the garment hang dead straight. Today's fashions require a more fluid approach.

Choice of design area

Although garments may be entirely bead-covered, certain areas are especially suitable for the application of bead embroidery: necklines, collars, cuffs, revers, waist and hip bands, yokes, shoulders, pockets, facings and hems. These areas are more likely to be constructed with a second layer of fabric, stiffened or interfaced. Heavy beading is to be avoided where it can be sat on or where it can rub. Gathers or folds look best with only a sprinkling of fine beads.

The beadwork should look as though it grows out from the background fabric rather than added as an afterthought, especially if the beadwork is combined with hand or machine embroidery. Work a series of small design samples and use the most pleasing of these as a basis for the actual embroidery. Save these samples for future reference.

The design needs to be related to the shape of the area to be beaded. Work linear or border designs along edges, and curved designs to fit collars. Adapt

44 Design areas on dress suitable for the inclusion of bead embroidery.

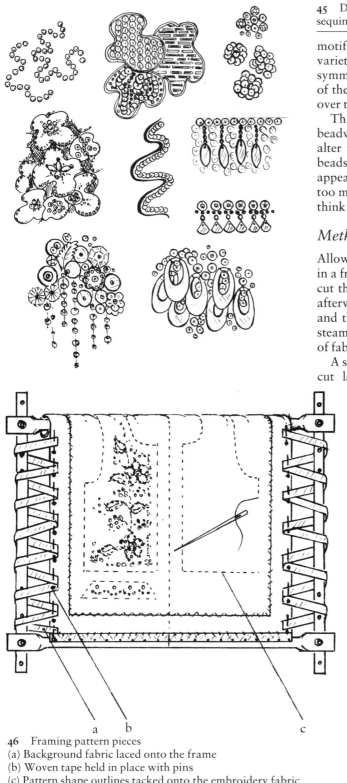

45   Design ideas using a variety of bugles, beads and sequins.

motifs, such as a flower with trailing stems, to fill a variety of spaces. The beading does not have to be symmetrical. The flower could twine from one side of the garment to the other, or trail from the front over to the back.

This type of design needs careful planning. The beadwork adds colour and raised texture which will alter the balance of the design. The way that the beads and sequins reflect the light will change the appearance. It is easy to get carried away and apply too many beads. The time to stop is just before you think the work is finished.

Method of work

Allow extra fabric as the beadwork is to be worked in a frame. If the area to be beaded is small enough, cut the garment pattern pieces out first and frame afterwards. A circular frame may mark some fabrics and this ring mark cannot always be removed by steaming. If you have any doubts, frame a test piece of fabric and leave for 24 hours before removing it.

A small area such as a pocket flap or a cuff can be cut larger than the finished pattern piece and

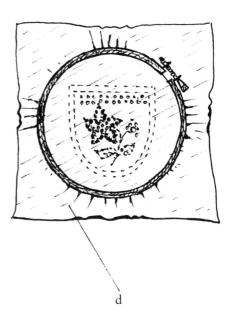

46   Framing pattern pieces
(a) Background fabric laced onto the frame
(b) Woven tape held in place with pins
(c) Pattern shape outlines tacked onto the embroidery fabric
(d) Embroidery fabric held in a ring frame with pocket outlines marked

1 Some of the types of beads and sequins available today: round beads in small plastic tubes and round plastic phials; *(at the back)* knitting beads in long plastic tubes; *(centre front)* tubular clay beads and wound glass beads made by Henry Spooner; *(left)* assorted sequins; *(right)* assorted bugle beads.

2 *Opposite page* Detail of shoulder decoration. Epaulette with beaded fringe, close-packed beads, sequins and gemstones. *(Joyce Law. Embroiderers' Guild Collection, 1983)*

3 *(Below)* Spray-dyed, machine-quilted, beaded sampler with detached leaves. Worked in metallic threads with the addition of small bronze beads. *(Sue Rangeley)*

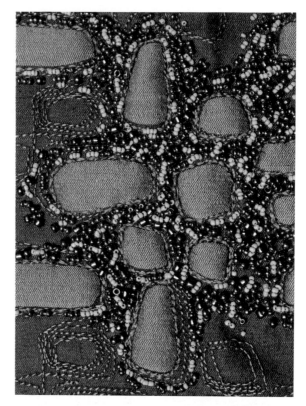

4 *(Right)* 'Blue Pools'. Massed beads on Schiffli machine-embroidered fabric with areas of trapunto quilting. *(Angela Thompson)*

5 Sheaf of corn on an altar frontal designed by Jane Lemon for the church of St John the Baptist, Wellington, Somerset. Ridged beads in gold and groups of bronze beads represent the ripe corn. *(Worked by Jane Lemon with Catherine Talbot)*

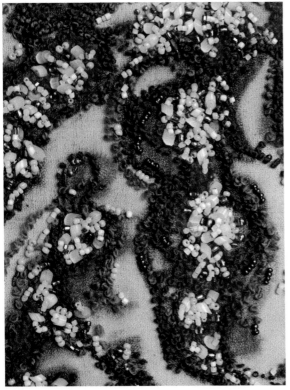

6 *(Above)* On the left, embroidered hanging bag with pockets decorated with cowrie shells. From Madhya Pradesh, Northern India. *(Author's collection)* On the right, hanging pocket with applied patchwork and bead decoration. *(Designed and made by Joan Appleton Fisher)*

7 'Forgotten Planet'. Detail of panel. Transfer dyes with Cornely machine loop stitching and massed beads. *(Angela Thompson)*

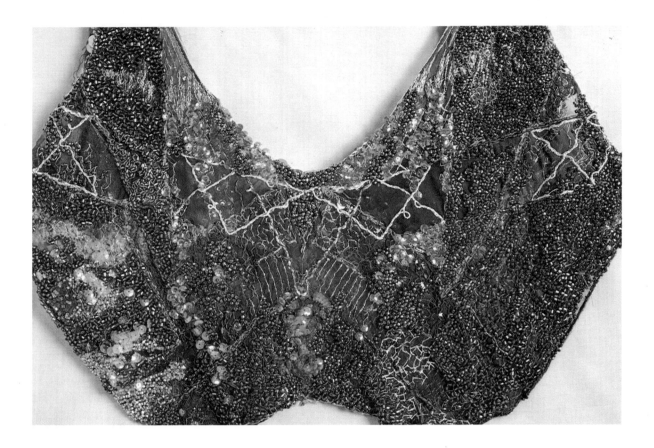

8 Evening bodice front. Sequins, bugle and cut beads, in different sizes, metallic threads tamboured to both sides of a georgette fabric base with the reverse beading showing through the layers. *(Paula Stypulkowski, Fashion Degree Course, Birmingham Polytechnic)*

9 Experimental design for a beaded screen in a
Birmingham nightclub. Large sequins tamboured onto
a background, covered with golden spotted voile with
applied velvet letters. *(Paula Stypulkowski)*

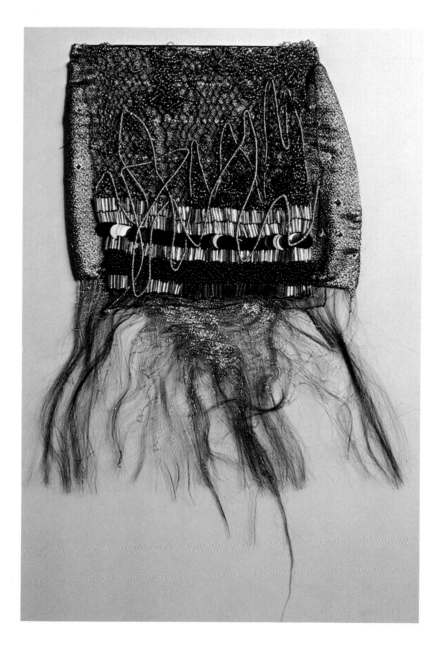

10 Experimental sample worked on organdie with
tamboured beads and stitchery forming a netted mesh.
(Paula Stypulkowski)

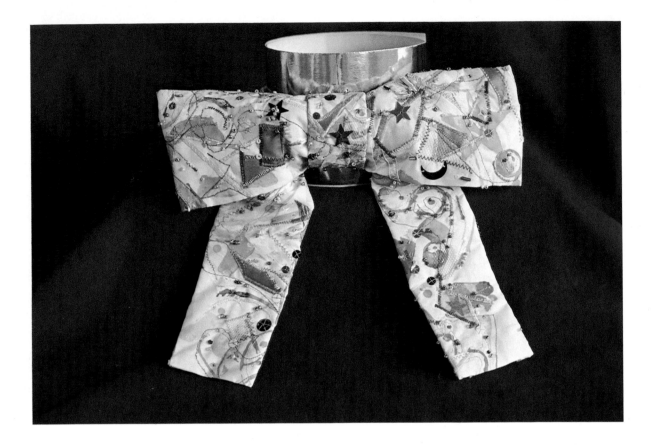

11 'Bow Tie'. City and Guilds embroidery beadwork
project. *(Mave Buckroyd)*

47 Bridal dress, back view. Machine embroidery with pearls on the low front and back neckline of the satin dress and the upper neckline of the voile section. (*Designed and made by Jennifer Stuart*)

48   Bridal dress (detail). Delicate free machine embroidery in fine metal thread with added seed pearls. (*Jennifer Stuart*)

applied to a backing which is then framed. Any necessary interfacing is applied at this stage. Free machine embroidery is better restricted to these areas if the ring frame is liable to mark.

Larger beaded areas are worked on the fabric before the pattern pieces are cut out. If you do not have a slate frame, make up a simple wooden frame to which the fabric can be stretched and stapled or pinned. The best method for very fine fabrics is to oversew the backed fabric over the frame edges. The garment pattern shapes are first marked by outlining with a tacking thread, then the bead design areas are marked out.

Seams

If the beading forms a continuous design across seamlines, make up a dress toile to be sure that the pattern pieces will fit properly. The bead design is interrupted at the seam allowance and the pattern is re-formed when the garment is sewn together. It may be necessary to hand stitch these seams with very small back stitches. Machine stitchery would crush the beadwork beneath the machine foot or result in a broken needle. The same sewing problems may arise when sewing facings, and it is advisable to hand stitch certain areas.

Pressing

It is almost impossible to press some seams on heavily beaded garments. Lay the garment with the bead side downwards and seam allowances opened up, onto a thick, soft towel. Lay cottonwool strips beneath the seam allowances and press the seam lightly with a steam iron just to set the stitches. Small areas of beadwork can be pinned out and stretched over dampened blotting paper if the fabric is suitable. Remove only when absolutely dry.

Bridal wear

Delicate beadwork of crystals and pearls will enhance a bridal gown, whether it is worked simply round the neck and cuffs, or encrusts the bodice and train for a Royal Wedding.

Design the bridal headdress in conjunction with the dress. In addition to sewn beadwork, beads can be threaded onto pliable wire and bent into decorative shapes. Jennifer Stuart has edged a dress neck and yoke with machine embroidery and tiny pearls to complement a headdress of larger pearls.

49 Bridal cap and veil with a border of seed pearls and bugle beads. Tiny seed pearls mark the centre veins of the detached, machine-embroidered leaves. (*Designed and made for the wedding of her daughter by Helen Archibald*)

Fashion accessories

Bags, purses and belts

The pattern shape is cut out with the seam allowances included. Apply to a stiffer fabric backing before framing and working the beads. The same applies to beaded neckbands, cuffs and hairbands.

Buttons and buckles

Allow extra fabric for covering a purchased button or buckle-mould and work the bead embroidery before assembling the parts.

Boots, shoes and slippers

Handmade slippers are beaded before making up, while purchased boots and shoes have to be beaded afterwards. Either use a curved needle to sew on the beads, or invest in a clamping tool to add jewels and crystals. Canvas-type shoes or boots are easier to sew and take on a new fashion dimension with added beads and jewels.

Plastic and transparent fabrics

Beads and sequins can be sewn onto these fabrics, or encased within them. Modern designers are using machine-knitted nylon monofilament to encase sequins, beads, braids and other small objects, either within a double fabric or in tiny pockets knitted into a garment.

Beads and sequins encased in transparent plastic, machine embroidered to form pockets, are made into see-through accessories, bags and purses. Take two layers of transparent fabric or plastic. Starting at the lower edge, sew three sides of a pocket before inserting tiny beads or sequins. Sew across the top of the pocket before starting the one above. The machine can be threaded with metallic yarn or with a heavier thread in the bobbin for a richer effect.

Use a Teflon-coated foot when machining plastic. If the foot persists in sticking, place a smear of oil on the top layer of plastic. Set to a larger stitch length and loosen the top tension a little.

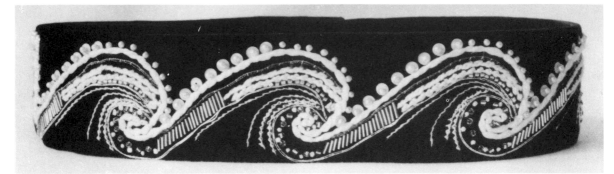

50 Beaded belt. Scroll design with embroidery stitches, pearls and bugle beads. (*Helen Archibald*)

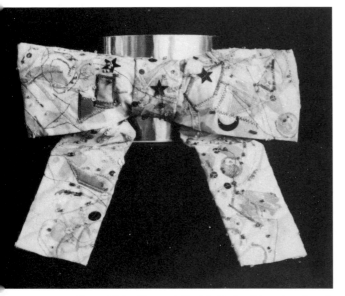

51 'Bow Tie'. City and Guilds Embroidery beadwork project. (*Mave Buckroyd, South Notts College of Further Education*)

Beaded knitwear and crochet

During the nineteenth century, beaded knitting and crochet became very popular. The beads were threaded onto the working yarn or thread beforehand, pushed up as required and knitted or crocheted into the stitch. Many beautiful beaded purses were decorated in this way.

This method is somewhat laborious and any patterned design had to be worked out beforehand with the beads threaded in the correct order. It is much easier to sew beads onto already knitted or crocheted fabric. The modern revival in high-fashion knitwear design has popularized the addition of beads, sequins and trimming to these garments.

Positioning

Sometimes beads are sewn at regular intervals to coincide with indentations or focal points within the pattern structure. On a plain surface the beadwork may form a single design element. Beaded motifs can be repeated at intervals.

The bead embroidery should in no way inhibit the stretch of crochet and knitted fabrics. Close-beaded patterns or motifs should be kept small in size, as it may be necessary to line this area. This applies to any purchased stretch fabric which is to be beaded, as well as to hand- or machine-knitted garments.

Sewing thread

If knitting beads are available, use the actual working yarn or thread. Untwist two- or three-ply yarn and split into a single thread to pass through smaller-sized beads. Natural yarns are not so strong as synthetic threads and can be strengthened by running a synthetic sewing thread in with the other. Small beads and sequins are sewn on using a synthetic or silk thread to tone with the garment colour. These threads have slightly more stretch than a cotton thread.

Needles

When sewing or beading knitwear or stretch fabrics, always use a blunt-pointed tapestry needle to slide between the loops. A sharp needle would split the threads. Tapestry needles have a long eye and come in various sizes.

How to sew the beads

A garment can be beaded before or after making up. If the design goes across the seams it should be beaded afterwards. Fasten on the sewing thread with a backstitch and then thread back to the bead position. Fasten off with a backstitch. Avoid running the thread between widely spaced beads as this will inhibit the garment stretch.

Reinforcing the knitwear

A stretch, iron-on interfacing may be applied to the

back of the knitted fabric before or after a beaded motif is worked. Avoid overpressing synthetic fabrics. Completely line any heavy outer garments, belts and bags with interfacing.

Knitted braids

Sew beads or sequins to the braid, either in the middle or down the edges. Thread a knitted rouleau through large beads and tie at intervals.

Soft sculpture

Add beads to experimental knitting and soft sculpture, preferably as part of the overall design.

Theatrical costume

Several of the methods which relate to fashion garments also apply to beadwork on theatrical costume. The difference is mainly one of scale. In the theatre everything has to be slightly larger than life, even for a television production.

The second consideration is one of cost. This includes not only the actual outlay on materials and bead ornaments, but also the time involved in the labour of sewing and making up. Many excellent substitutes have been found to represent the heavy beadwork and jewellery worn during the Tudor and Elizabethan periods.

The popularity of costume drama has provided scope for the designer. Stage costume is always viewed from a distance and needs a bold approach. In costume drama on television, it is a matter of deceiving the camera eye. Close-up shots need to be taken into consideration.

There is great demand for exotic beadwork in the popular entertainment industry. Musicians, singers, dancers, skaters, circus performers all love the glamour of beaded and sequinned costumes.

Some of these decorative ideas, in a less exaggerated form, are copied by the fashion industry. It is a process which has been going on for a long time. The nineteenth-century actress Sarah Bernhardt started a fashion for wearing dress bodices heavily beaded with gems and pearls. In the 1930s the glamour of the film star was emulated; today we are influenced by television.

Heavy beadwork for theatrical costume

Plastic objects

Pieces from model kits or parts designed for industrial or domestic use are ideal for mock-jewellery. Different-sized objects can be glued together and any unwanted protrusions cut or filed off before spray painting with metallic colours. Small holes are drilled to aid sewing onto fabric. If they are to be strung, they need weighting by glueing or

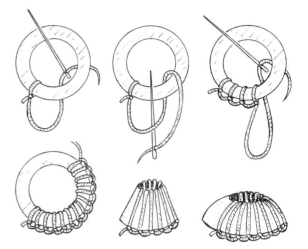

52 Heavy beadwork: covering different-shaped rings with Hedebo buttonhole stitch.

taping some small heavy metal object or coin behind to make them hang correctly.

Hardware

Heavier parts from hardware shops or mechanical stores can be sprayed to look more realistic, but are difficult to sew in place. Small metal or ceramic parts for industrial use make excellent 'jewels' or they may be strung as beads. Chains of different types are available and are kept whole, or broken into their separate parts which are sewn as decorative beads.

Rings and washers come in all shapes and sizes. Sew them down singly to encase a jewel stone, or place over a centre of gold or silver card. Wind them with metallic cords and shiny ribbon or twist bead strings over padding to give a rich effect.

Use the Hedebo buttonhole technique to cover rings with soft metallic knitting thread. Tie the thread end over the ring with a knot to hold in place. Hold the knotted thread end in the left hand between finger and thumb, together with the base of the ring. With a threaded tapestry needle come up from below the ring, through the centre hole. This makes a loop. Next bring the needle up through this loop from below and pull tight (one stitch formed).

Repeat until the ring is full and fasten off firmly. Many different shapes, providing they are basically circular and have a central hole, can be covered this way. Apply to the background with fine, strong matching thread.

Jewellery findings

Break cheap necklaces up into parts. Oxfam shops and jumble sales are a good source of the older, heavier type of bead. Save sewing time by stringing

53 Theatrical embroidery motif to be repeated down eighteenth-century jacket front. Sample using crochet braid of soft Lurex yarn and applied soft metallic cord. Large metallic button and sequins added afterwards. (*Angela Thompson*)

beads or metal findings in pattern order and couch this string down at intervals.

Beads combined with braids

Space out strings of beads or other objects and couch onto decorative braids. If these are to be applied to the costume garments by machine, keep the decoration to the centre.

Effective braids can be crocheted from soft metallic knitting threads and used to surround areas of sequins or beading. A small mechanical french knitter, called a Tricotin, will produce yards of tubular knitted rouleau braid as fast as you can turn the handle.

Purchased sequin braid and beaded trimmings are applied by couching down at intervals. Apply them in rows, or twist to make frogged patterns.

'Chocolate-box' cord

These heavy, synthetic gold and silver cords are sold by the reel, or you may like to collect and save chocolate-box and gift wrappings. Combine them with heavy jewellery findings, or apply by zigzag machine stitch before adding beaded braids or sequin strips.

Pasta

Pasta shapes can be sprayed and substituted for heavy beadwork, especially in the context of children's drama and amateur theatricals. This method of decoration is only temporary – if the pasta gets damp, it will go mouldy. Cut, rolled and glued corrugated card, or cut and shaped polystyrene are more permanent.

Finer beadwork for costume and evening wear

Crystals and jewels

Those which have a flat base should be glued into position. Avoid areas that are subject to much wear or the gems may catch. Clamped gemstones are ideal in this context.

Iron-on diamanté and pearls

As well as being a useful addition to dress embroidery, this type of decoration comes into its own when used for theatrical work. Strips of diamanté or pearls may be cut into lengths or used as individual stones. They are resistant to dry cleaning and washable up to 60° Centigrade. The following instructions were given to the author by Ellis and Farrier Limited:

1. Remove the white paper from the back of the diamanté or pearls and place in the required position on the material. The transparent cover is slightly tacky and will hold them in position until fixed.

54 'Dragon'. Panel, metal threads and applied gold kid, with beads and sequins. (*Marie Roper, Advanced City and Guilds Embroidery*)

2. Adjust the temperature of a domestic iron as for wool/cotton, turn the material to the reverse side, cover with a piece of cloth and press with a strong pressure on a normal ironing board. It is important to allow the material to cool before turning it to the right side. Remove the transparent cover strip.

The use of a steam iron may assist adhesion on heavy materials. Take care that the diamanté or pearls do not penetrate the depressions on the surface of the steam iron or the necessary pressure cannot be exerted.

Beads with metal thread embroidery

Metal threads, applied to a background fabric, or added to raised and padded areas, are used both for ecclesiastical and secular embroideries. Their glowing quality is especially suited to church embroidery. Both beads and sequins help to enrich the embroidery and are used to give weight and contrast to the areas of metal thread work. Metallic beads, gold or silver, come in a variety of sizes and shapes.

Metal threads

There are many different types of metal thread available. They fall into two general categories. Those which have a silk or thread core with thin sheet metal wound round are held down with couching stitches. These metal threads can be plain, twisted or crimped, single or many-stranded.

The other type are called purls and are made from very finely drawn wire twisted round to give a hollow centre, like a tiny spring. Smooth purl is shiny, rough purl slightly duller. Check purl is almost four-sided in cross section. The purls are cut into very small lengths and applied as you would a bead. The main difference is that they are springy and, unlike a bead, can be made to curve slightly or stand proud of the fabric.

Couched threads

Most metal threads are held onto the surface of the fabric with couching stitches. Only fine threads are taken through the cloth. The metal threads are laid double with even couching stitches going over the two parallel threads. Afterwards, ends are taken through to the reverse of the fabric, using a large-eyed chenille needle.

Application

There is a long tradition in the use of beads, bugles

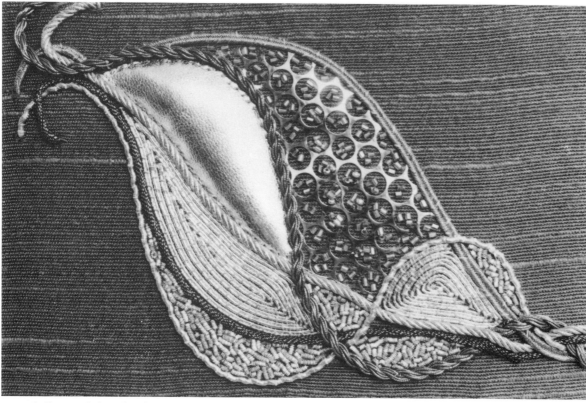

55 'Shell'. Metal thread embroidery with padded gold kid, applied cords, check purl, beads and sequin waste. (*Angela Thompson*)

and sequins together with metal thread embroidery, especially in India and the Middle East.

An image robe, in the Victoria and Albert Museum, made for a figure of the Virgin Mary or for a saint, is cut from fabric of a possible Indian origin. It is embroidered with trailing stems and exotic flower and cone shapes in metal thread and flat spangles or sequins. The stems are delineated with overlapping spangles; other spangles are attached by short lengths of check purl either side of a central leaf stalk. Moonstones are surrounded with a number of short lengths of purl. Silver metal threads radiate out to a spangled arc. Another piece of embroidery has larger, flat sequins sewn down with two separate twists of rough purl, to give a braided effect.

The 1986 exhibition 'Hats from India' at the Victoria and Albert Museum provided many examples. Among these were flat sequins overlapped in double outline, held by the leaf-vein centres in short lengths of check purl; rosettes in a similar technique radiating outwards; and a crown from Lucknow had a scallop pattern outlined with

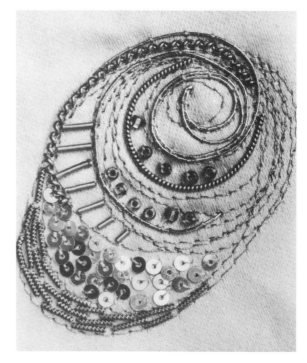

56 Metal thread embroidery sample with sequins. (*Marie Roper*)

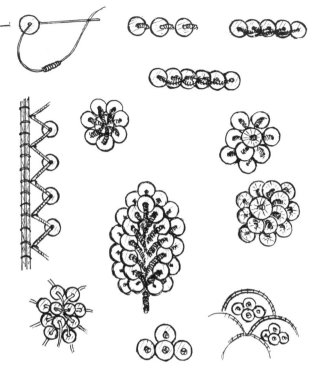

57 Metal thread
Various methods of sewing down flat sequins using cut purl
Sequins held with metal thread, straight stitches or french knots (*bottom*)

metal thread and infilled with spangles, each held with a french knot of gold metallic thread.

Also in the Victoria and Albert Museum is a beaded bodice and train from a dress designed by Doucet in 1897. It is embroidered with an exuberant mixture of metal thread, crystal and pearl beads, emerald and diamanté jewels in claw settings, and round and oval sequins. Bundles of fine metal thread are couched at intervals and surround large, chunky crystal bugles. Long pieces of rough purl hold down the oval-shaped sequins. Short lengths of check pearl surround each claw-set emerald. Double leaf shapes are outlined with couched metal thread bundles which are infilled with overlapping sequins. The effect is rich indeed.

Church embroidery

Unlike theatrical embroidery, ecclesiastical embroidery should look good both from a distance and at close quarters. It is not easy to achieve this balance.

During the Middle Ages beads could be substituted for gemstones on church vestments. The nuns from poorer convents were sometimes forced to sell their gems and replace them with bead embroidery. This type of work gradually became more popular as different kinds of beads became available.

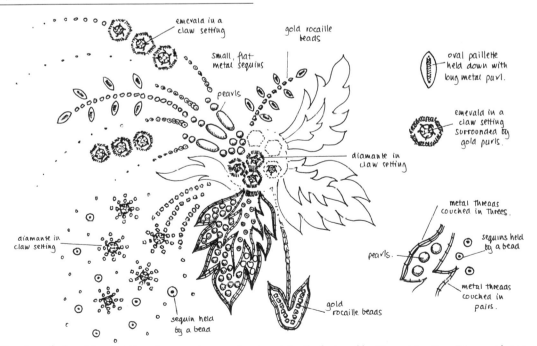

58 Sketches of a hand-beaded French court dress and train originally designed by Doucet in 1897. Diamanté, gemstones, pearls, beads and sequins combined with metal thread embroidery. (*Victoria and Albert Museum*)

59 Beaded cross with mirror centre, on a box lid. Beads incorporated in the stitchery of raised chain band worked over shaped polystyrene. (*Jane Lemon*)

Design and application

Sew beads on their own or work them together with the metal thread embroidery. The areas and articles chosen for bead embroidery follow the same rules as those for metal thread embroidery. Take into consideration whether the embroidered article is to be cleaned or washed; whether it is to be subjected to much handling and if the purpose for which the article is made renders it suitable for raised embroidery of any kind.

Altar furnishings

The frontal cloth provides plenty of space for decoration. It hangs from the altar front or can be attached to the cloth which covers the altar top. Separate embroidered bands may be superimposed at either end and give further scope for embroidery. The laudian or throw-over cloth for free-standing altars is normally embroidered at the front.

Pulpit-falls, banners and burses

These form an excellent background for the addition of beads and metal thread. Pulpit-falls and banners are heavily lined to make them hang properly, while the burse is embroidered on the front and laced over card to form a stiff, hinged cover.

Vestments

Traditionally the stole and maniple are embroidered at the ends or along the lower edges. Both are made from long narrow strips of fabric. The stole hangs around the neck, straight for a bishop, crossed for a priest. The maniple hangs over the forearm.

Daphne Nicholson, in her informative booklet, *Symbolism, Colour and Embroidery in Hereford Cathedral*, tells us that a wider stole will be adopted to wear over the new cassock alb and this can be decorated over its full length.

The chasuble

This outer vestment, which has altered in shape over the centuries, is worn by the celebrant. In the past the chasuble was heavily embroidered. A simpler form may have embroidered bands which are called orphreys.

The cope

The cope is a cloak-like outer garment which is fastened at the front by a clasp called a morse. Both the cope and the morse lend themselves to sumptuous embroidery. For a plainer cope the embroidery could be limited to the orphrey bands bordering the front edges.

The mitre

This stiffened headdress is worn by the bishop together with the cope and is generally embroidered to match it.

Beaded stitchery

Beaded stitches

Beading can form an integral part of free stitchery although technically every sewn bead is a beaded stitch. In the present context it is the stitch itself which is of importance, rather than being just a means of holding down the bead. Different types of bead can be threaded onto the working thread and used to form part of the stitch.

Straight stitches

All straight stitches are suitable for the addition of beads. This includes the whole family of crossed stitches. Thread beads onto the straight part of stitches such as Cretan, herringbone, Romanian and buttonhole.

Looped stitches

Include beads with some of the half-looped stitches such as feather or fly stitch and into the loop of buttonhole stitch. Beads may be threaded onto the loops of chained stitches and worked into the formation of knotted stitches, but this can give a lopsided effect.

Thread beads onto ladder stitches or onto the arms of vandyke, alternating the beads or placing them at random intervals. String a bead onto the connecting thread between the knots in coral stitch.

Most stitches will take an added bead even if this means exaggerating some part of the stitch.

Suitable beads and threads

The scale of the embroidery is determined by the size of hole in the beads. Most beads have very small holes, and this can restrict the choice of thread. Larger-scale beads are available for craft work and thick yarns may be threaded through easily. This tends to limit the range of threads by excluding those of medium thickness. Knitting beads will take a medium to fine yarn while some necklace beads or

60   Free stitchery: sample of knitting beads on Cretan stitch. (*Jane Davies*)

those sold to laceworkers may have slightly larger holes. It is worth searching for them.

How to sew

The bead is slipped onto the embroidery thread after the needle has come up through the cloth and before the final part of thc stitch is completed. It is necessary to work some samples to see if the beads are suitable for use within the chosen stitch. Some beads will not lie flat. Try including them in a different part of the stitch, or within an alternative version of the stitch.

Sequins

These are threaded onto the stitch in the same way. Some stitches may not be suitable as the sequins are liable to twist over. The reflective qualities of this effect are used to advantage in experimental embroidery.

Combining beaded stitches with plain stitches

The added beads need careful placing within the stitch design. Thinly spread beadwork may look disjointed. On the other hand, too many beads will hide the stitchery. It is possible to add beaded stitchery; but odd beads cannot be cut out without destroying the stitch structure.

Design ideas and texture

Collect cuttings from magazines, especially those of foliage, or of natural features like rock formations or sea-coral. Be prepared to experiment with different bead and stitch combinations to see which one will best express the design in mind. Limit the type of stitch used. One-stitch embroidery can be most expressive.

Beaded canvas embroidery

Berlin woolwork patterns were first imported to England during the early 1830s. They became extremely popular with the newly leisured class of ladies, wives of wealthy merchants and industrialists. By the middle of the century beads were added, including pearls, sequins and cut-steel as well as the more common seed bead. Beaded work in white, black and shades of grey, sometimes on a stitched wool background, was called 'grisaille' and often chosen for handscreens, footstools and firescreens. Other items decorated with beads included banners, bell-pulls, watch pockets, wristlets, bags, slippers and cushions. This type of embroidery was popular well into the 1870s.

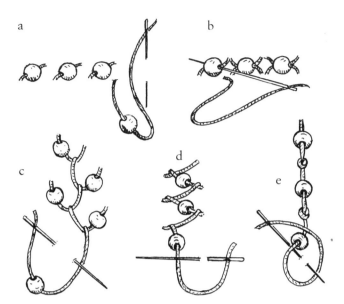

61 Free beaded stitches
(a) Beaded cross stitch, stage one
(b) Beaded cross stitch, stage two, going through the bead a second time on the return journey
(c) Beaded feather stitch
(d) Beaded Cretan stitch
(e) Beaded coral stitch

62 Mid-Victorian beaded canvas embroidery, with some tent stitch in yarn and beads slanting in different directions. (*Museum of Costume and Textiles, Nottingham*)

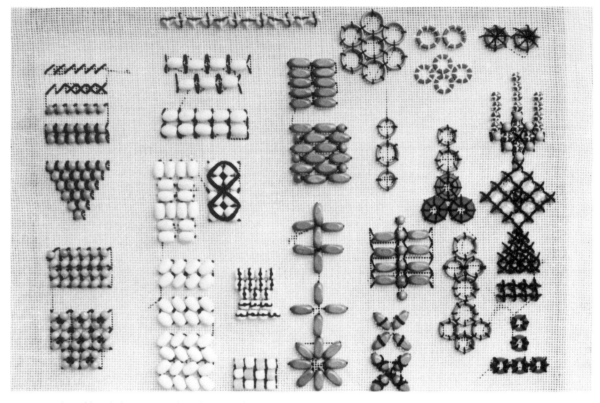

63 Sampler of beaded canvas embroidery stitches.
(*Sean Carroll*)

In her book, *How to do Beadwork*, first published in 1904 and reprinted by Dover Publications, Mary White writes: 'In the present revival of beadwork wonderful specimens of bead-embroidered canvas have been made.' She goes on to tell us how '... garland designs are wrought in finest beads of harmonious colours on iridescent or pearly backgrounds, sometimes flecked with tiny patterns of gold.'

More recently Diana Keay, who is a member of the Practical Study Group of the Embroiderers' Guild, has redirected our attention to this type of bead work.

Modern application

In the past the beaded canvas work was generally confined to tent stitch embroidery. There is no reason why other canvas work stitches should not be adapted for beaded canvas embroidery. Much of the Victorian work was entirely bead-covered. This gave a stiff look to the work. It was very heavy and only suitable for use on certain items. Other pieces had the central design motifs worked in beads and the background filled in with tent stitch. Today there is a more fluid approach.

Beaded canvas embroidery stitches

Beaded tent stitch
The embroidery is worked onto double-thread or Penelope canvas. The beads sit neatly on the intersection of the double-thread pairs. The beads should all be sewn in the same direction unless this variation is a deliberate design feature. They face in the opposite direction to which they are sewn. If you want beads and the background tent stitches all to face the same way, reverse the beading stitch.

Round- or rocaille-beads of even shape and size are used. The beads should lie neatly together and not overcrowd one another.

Threads   Sew with a strong silk, cotton or synthetic thread such as polyester which tones in with the beads. Wax the thread for ease of sewing.

Method of work   The beads may be sewn in rows across, or in lines up the canvas. For larger areas, keep to one method only. Always start each row from the same end even if it means fastening on again. Otherwise, turn the canvas upside-down on alternate rows to keep the beads slanting the same way.

Fasten on the thread by tying to the canvas before threading through to the starting position. Make two back stitches within the canvas and come up through a space. Thread a bead onto the needle.

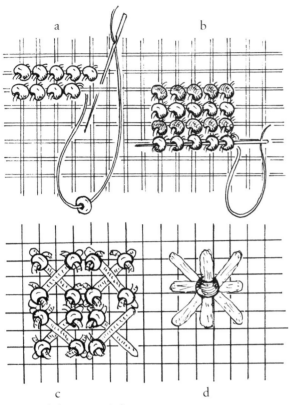

64 Beaded canvas stitches
(a) Working beaded tent stitch on double-thread canvas
(b) Securing the beads by threading back through the holes
(c) Beaded rice stitch on single canvas
(d) Smyrna or double cross stitch with a large central bead on the final stitch

65 Section of the sampler showing on the left the use of industrial ceramic parts donated by Morgan Macroc Ltd, Stourport-on-Severn. (*Sean Carroll*)

Push the bead down onto the canvas and make a diagonal stitch into the next space to the right above the first thread intersection. Sew three or four more similar beaded stitches. Slide the needle back through these beads to make a lock stitch. Either start a new row, or thread back to the working position.

Beaded cross stitches

It is not necessary to work beaded cross stitches onto double-thread canvas unless you wish to combine them with beaded tent stitch.

The actual embroidery thread is used to secure the beads which should have a large enough hole for the thread to pass through twice. Stranded embroidery threads or tapestry yarns may be divided for this purpose.

The beaded cross stitch is worked in two stages. Fasten on at the left, slip the needle through the bead and make the first diagonal of the cross stitch towards the right. Repeat for each half stitch along the row. The second part of the cross stitch is completed on the return journey working from right to left with the needle passing through the bead a second time. The cross is thus secured within the bead.

Beads can be threaded onto other crossed stitches during the working process. Slip a smaller bead onto each crossed corner of rice stitch. Alternate the bead positions on upright or on double cross. Thread a bead onto long-legged cross or the diagonal of Italian cross.

Many other canvas stitches are suitable for use with beading including the flat stitches. The upright threads of sheaf stitch are effectively held in place by a bead.

66 'Beetle'. Three-dimensional canvas embroidery with beads incorporated in the stitchery. (*Designed and made by Pip Noble, City and Guilds Embroidery*)

Design ideas and application

It is possible to include beads in many of the designs suitable for canvas embroidery. However, their inclusion should give meaning to the design. Sometimes the beads are confined to certain areas or added as highlights where their reflective quality gives interpretation to such subjects as a butterfly's wings, water or frost crystals.

The canvas-stitched background need not be limited to tent stitch when worked on the double-thread canvas. Other canvas embroidery stitches will give added interest; but tent stitch should be worked as an infill around the beaded areas.

Padding and appliqué

Applied felt, leather or gold kid is sewn down onto the canvas before either the beading or the canvas stitches are worked. A padding of small felt pieces, each one slightly larger than the one beneath, may be sewn onto the canvas before the gold or silver kid is applied on top. The beads are sewn close enough to be worked into the edges of these applied sections. An alternative method is to apply the piece, but leave a gap into which stuffing is inserted before it is closed.

The design is traced onto the canvas with a waterproof felt pen from the drawing which is placed beneath. Canvas embroidery should be worked in a frame and stretched afterwards if necessary. Panels are mounted over hardboard and laced up the back.

Beadweaving techniques

Beadweaving, or bead looming as it is sometimes called, is worked by many different races of people around the world. The availability of the even-sized trade beads gave regularity to the technique and their bright colours were translated into geometric designs.

Traditional beadweaving is worked on a small loom with the fine, lengthways warp threads held slightly apart at the ends. There should be an odd number of warp threads as the beads lie between them. The working, or weft thread is passed

67 Amazonian Indian apron. Work in progress on a bow-loom with the bottom warp threads tied in groups to a lashed cross-piece. (*On exhibition display at the Museum of Mankind, 1986–7*)

through a long beading needle and secured by tying onto the first outside warp thread.

Beads equalling the number of warp spaces are threaded onto the needle and slipped down. They are held from beneath and each one is pushed up into position between a warp thread. The working thread goes over the top of the last warp thread and is then passed back through all the beads. They are thus secured with a thread both over and under the warp. Narrow braids are easier to work.

Beaded needleweaving

Beadweaving has been combined with embroidery

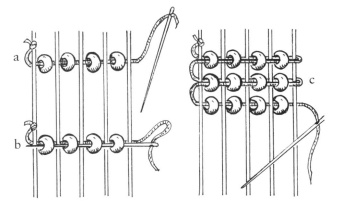

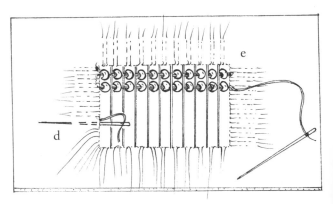

68 Beaded needleweaving
(a) Pushing up the strung beads between the warp threads
(b) Taking the needle over the warp threads and back through the beads
(c) Beadweaving in progress
(d) Darning back the threads withdrawn from fabric
(e) Beaded needleweaving between the warp threads

in the past, forming part of needleweaving techniques.

In the Museum of Mankind in London there is an apron made of coarsely woven cloth which would have been worn by an Indian warrior from the Amazon area of South America. Alternate warp threads have been taken out in the central area and the spaces filled in using larger-scale beads, all in a neutral colour. Another apron is part woven: the warp threads were stretched across a bow-loom, and coloured beads on the weft thread were incorporated between each of the warp threads.

Mary White, in *How to do Beadwork*, describes a '. . . decoration for a burlap curtain', made with '. . . the large glass beads that come in round wooden boxes for kindergarten work'. Here the weft threads are withdrawn at the top of a deep hem. The beads are pushed up into the spaces between groups of three threads. As the fabric is soft, the threads sink between the beads, which are sewn into geometric patterns.

Needleweaving methods

Choose a soft, evenweave fabric such as linen, furnishing fabric or hessian. Mark the area where the threads are to be withdrawn by outlining with a tacking thread. Using a sharp pair of scissors, cut the weft threads down the centre of this area, being careful not to cut the warp. Tease out the threads from the centre and weave each one back into the sides. An alternative method is to buttonhole down the sides of the area and cut these threads close to the buttonhole stitches.

The beads are woven in using the same technique described for bead looming. If the beads are large, place them between groups of threads, or remove alternate threads as in the Amazonian apron.

Designs

Although this method lends itself to geometric patterns, the work can be planned to include needlewoven thread stitches with the beads.

Free needleweaving

This is a type of stitchery with the foundation, or warp threads, sewn onto background fabric. These threads can vary in length and radiate from a central point before being woven across, using the same working thread. It is possible to slip beads onto the foundation stitches before they are woven across. The beads are held in position by the needleweaving. The embroidery should be worked in a frame, and the finished work stretched over a mount in

69 Beaded needleweaving, work in progress, showing the weft threads withdrawn and every third warp thread left with the others withdrawn. Wooden beads from the 1930s. (*Jane Davies*)

order to keep the long threads at tension. Edith John's book, *Needleweaving*, is a useful source of stitch information.

Needleweaving over beads

Large beads which have too fine a hole, making it impossible to pass the embroidery thread through, may be held down with free needleweaving stitchery. Hold the bead temporarily in position with double-sided sticky tape. Do not be tempted to use glue, which is bound to show. Hold the bead in place with the foundation threads. Work needleweaving stitches across and anchor the thread into the fabric at intervals to prevent the bead from slipping. Other small objects, shells, seed heads or pieces of bark are held in a similar manner.

70   Free needleweaving: sample incorporating wooden beads with the stitchery. (*Jane Davies*)

Shisha work

The pieces of mirror glass are held onto the fabric with a network of surrounding stitches. The mirror is held down with the left thumb. Bring the thread up from beneath the cloth and lay two separated parallel threads across one way. Two more threads are laid across the opposite way, taking the needle under and round each intersection. For greater security, lay another four threads across diagonally. This framework is stitched into with a Hedebo buttonhole stitch going through the network and into the cloth (fig. 71).

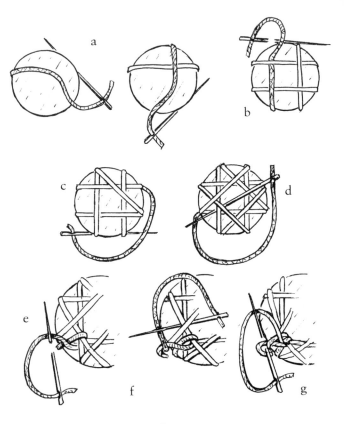

71   How to work shisha stitch
(a) First hold the shisha glass piece in place by laying four threads across at right-angles to one another, stitching through the cloth
(b) Slip the needle under the last thread intersection and take a small stitch into the cloth at the circle top left
(c) Make four more stitches across to form a lattice, the final one into the cloth
(d) Come out a short distance away and use the working thread to buttonhole stitch over the lattice of threads
(e) Make a short buttonhole stitch into the cloth
(f) Buttonhole over the lattice
(g) Buttonhole into both the previous loop and the cloth. Repeat all the way round

Drawn thread work

The fabric used for drawn thread work may be finer than that recommended for needleweaving. Threads are withdrawn from the fabric and neatened in a similar manner. Clumps of warp threads are drawn together with encircling stitches using an embroidery thread. These clumps may be subdivided to form patterns during the work.

The beads are first threaded onto the working tie-thread. They are pushed up one at a time and included in the tie-stitch, or several may be strung between the tie-threads.

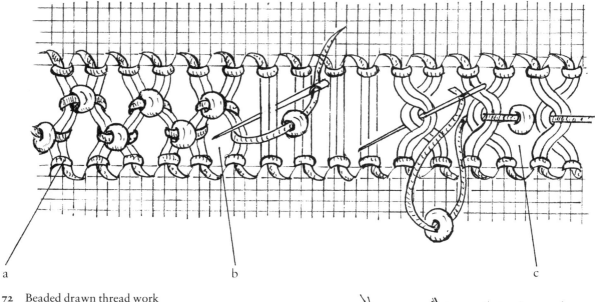

72 Beaded drawn thread work
(a) Hemstitched edge on fabric with weft threads withdrawn
(b) Lattice border with beads included in the binding stitch
(c) Twisted border with beads threaded between the twists

Net beading

The beads are included in the meshes of the net rather than being sewn on top of it. This is a Victorian method rather like beaded canvas embroidery in that it is adaptable for geometric patterns. It is worked onto hexagonal-mesh net. This is not easy to obtain in a size large enough to accommodate the beads. Present-day bobbin lace workers could make their own net backgrounds to the required size.

The beads are sewn across the rows of mesh, with flat edges of the hexagon at top and bottom. The securing stitch is taken into the top of the hexagon. Each beaded row is half-dropped as the hexagons fit into one another. The pattern cannot be worked from a square grid.

Net darning

Thread the beads onto the decorative darning thread before taking a stitch. The beads should be small in order not to dominate the work, but with holes large enough for the thread to pass through. Crystal beads give sparkle and lightness to the work. In some instances, sequins may be added within star stitches.

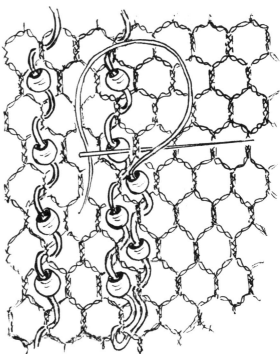

73 Beading on bobbin net mesh. The beaded working thread is taken horizontally from left to right beneath each mesh upright in the vertical row. This allows a bead to sit within each hexagonal mesh.

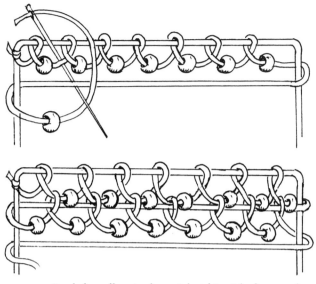

74 Beaded needlepoint lace. A bead is picked up on the working thread each time a needlepoint lace stitch is worked into the row above.

Beaded needlepoint lace

In the Victoria and Albert Museum there is a little pulled work and darning stitched mat that once belonged to Mrs Lewis Day. Both Lewis F. Day author of *Art in Needlework*, and his wife collected textiles. The origin of this mat is not known. It is decorated with needlepoint lace patterned with beads. The beads are 'off-set' as they form part of the needlepoint stitchery. The lace, which is an added decoration to the hem, is worked in a pattern of triangular points. All is finished with a fringe. Little birds and tiny flowers form the bead pattern which is made by threading a bead onto the loop of the needlepoint lace stitch.

To make beaded needlepoint lace, thread is first laid across the design area. This is buttonholed into, leaving a series of loops. A second thread is laid across in the same direction. The next set of buttonhole stitches is worked into both this thread and the loops of the row above. This stitch is called corded filling. It gives a firm foundation for the beads and prevents them from slipping within the pattern. The beads are picked up on the working thread and incorporated with the buttonhole stitches.

Many other needlepoint lace stitches, which are either looped stitches or buttonhole stitches, are suitable for the inclusion of beads. Modern versions of needlepoint lace are worked with thicker threads, including heavy yarns, and this would allow the use of larger beads. The word 'needlepoint' means 'needle stitch' and is often used in the context of canvas embroidery which is also stitched with a needle. The term 'needlepoint tapestry' came from the need to differentiate between woven and hand-stitched wall coverings.

7 | *Beaded smocking and beaded quilting*

Beaded smocking

Smocking lends itself to the inclusion of beads, both as an addition to the work and as an integral part of the stitchery. Smocking has developed from its purely practical use to become a branch of embroidery in its own right.

Traditional smocked garments were constructed from a series of rectangular pattern pieces. When cloth was handwoven the precious fabric was cut to obviate as much waste as possible. The extra fullness was controlled by gathers held with smocking stitches. These allow for some elasticity in the smocked parts, essential when the garment was worn by manual workers.

The smocking stitches are not only practical; they are also very decorative. The patterns on the smocks varied from area to area, but were not necessarily linked with the trade or occupation of the wearer.

In the Victorian era it was fashionable to clothe children in copies of adult or workman's dress. The sailor suit is a well-known instance. This led to a scaled-down version of the adult smock. Later, areas of smocking were included in children's garments, and its use gradually spread to adult wear.

In the costume section of the Birmingham City Museum and Art Gallery, a wedding dress of the

75 Experimental smocking sample showing strung pearls, strung sequins and added beads. Made by the author during a workshop tutored by the late Margaret Thom, early 1970s.

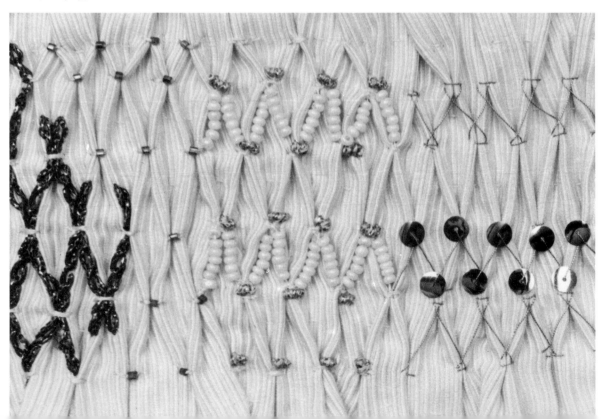

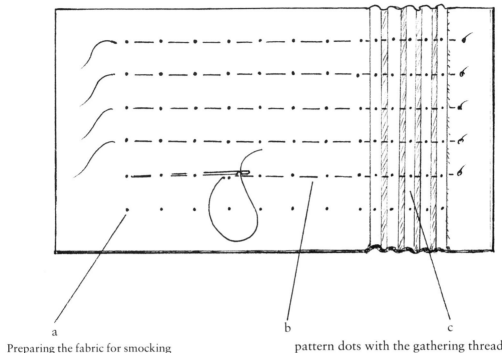

76   Preparing the fabric for smocking
(a) Smocking dots
(b) Gathering threads
(c) Gathered fabric reeds

1880s is decorated with pearls on honeycomb smocking. This forms a feature on the sleeves and on alternating panels set into the skirt. A matching purse, made in the same cream silk satin, is also embroidered with pearls on honeycomb smocking.

During the early 1920s, blouses were worn with decorative areas of smocking on yokes, cuffs and even on hip belts. Another revival in the late 1930s popularized the Hungarian peasant-type blouse worked in coloured silks.

In 1972 the late Margaret Thom produced a book called *Smocking in Embroidery* which featured the use of beads on smocking as well as their inclusion in the actual stitch structure.

The Smocking Group of the Embroiderers' Guild has been formed to foster an interest in smocking and to co-ordinate the talents of embroiderers. This recent revival, both in the making and wearing of the traditional-type smock, has led to the inclusion of smocking on clothing and fashion accessories such as bags and purses.

Ready-smocked work with beads or sequins added afterwards

The smocked structure is formed by the gathering of fabric into ridged folds called reeds, pipes or tubes. The reeds are formed by picking up rows of regular pattern dots with the gathering thread. The farther apart the dots, the deeper the folds will be. Ready-printed transfer paper with a grid of dots is ironed onto the reverse side of the fabric. Another method is to use patterned fabric already printed with dots, tiny flower clumps, stripes, checks or ridges.

Method
Use a strong thread for making the gathers. Knot firmly at the top right of the working area and pick up each tiny dot with the needle, working from right to left. Gather each row of dots before gently easing the fabric folds along the gathering threads. Keep all the gathering threads of equal length. At the row ends, place a pin between every two pairs and wind the surplus threads round each pin, or tie together in pairs. This gives security to the threads, which are removed when the smocking is finished.

Threads and needles
Choose from twisted embroidery thread, coton-à-broder, perlé, soft linen thread, or stranded cotton. Other finer threads may be substituted when beaded smocking is worked. A fine crewel embroidery needle with a longer eye will accommodate the thicker threads without distorting the fabric.

Stitches
The smocking stitches are worked onto the right side of the fabric starting at the left-hand side. The fabric reed is picked up with a horizontal stitch keeping each one the same depth for even results.

The traditional stitches were variations of stem stitch, also referred to as outline stitch. These can be

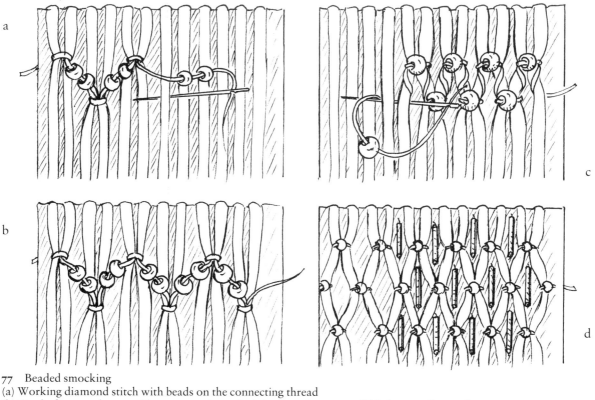

77 Beaded smocking
(a) Working diamond stitch with beads on the connecting thread
(b) Worked across the row. The next row is worked the opposite way up. This forms a diamond
(c) Vandyke stitch, with beads on the tie-thread
(d) Beaded honeycomb stitch, the connecting thread taken behind the reeds. Bugle beads sewn into the hollows afterwards

worked in straight lines across, or in wave or trellis formation. Cable stitch is based on alternating stem stitch and is worked single or double.

Honeycomb and chevron stitches, which have more elasticity, came later and were always popular for use on children's clothing. These simple stitches are combined to produce other variations.

Adding the beads
The beads are sewn either onto the ridges of the reeds, or into the spaces made by the smocking stitches, between the reeds. Sew single beads up and down the ridges to form a pattern, or make little strings of beads and catch down at intervals. Alternate with longer bugle beads or rows of sequins.

The hollows between honeycomb stitch make an excellent siting for oval beads such as pearls or crystal drops. Insert the beads in geometric pattern order, or simply add them into alternate rows. Tuck a sequin, held down with a bead, into the hollows of diamond stitch.

Beads sewn with the working thread

In this technique the beads are sewn on during the actual working of the smocking stitches. If it is not possible to pass the embroidery thread through finer beads, use one of the following methods:
1. Work all the smocking stitches first with the smocking thread. Work the beaded smocking stitches afterwards using a finer thread.
2. Embroider the smocking with a finer thread incorporating the beads in the stitchery. Thin metallic cords are excellent for this purpose.

The method of work is the same in both instances. The bead or sequin is slipped onto the thread before the stitch is completed. Those stitches which have a long connecting thread passing across the reeds, such as diamond or cable, make a good support for the beads. Sew a single bead for honeycomb onto the horizontal stitch that connects the reeds.

Vary the number of beads or sequins or a mixture to suit the length of stitch. Vary the length and type of bead. Bugle beads work well in this context.

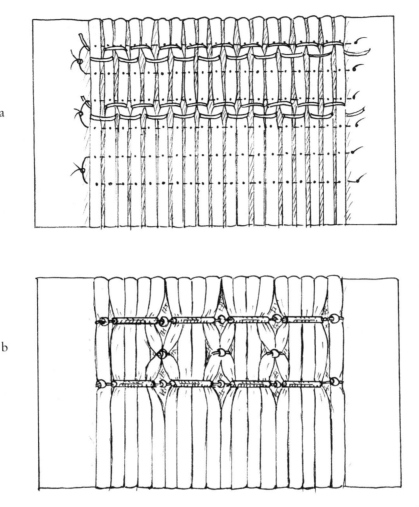

a

b

78   Reverse smocking on prepared reeds
(a) Rows of cable stitch worked onto the wrong side of the gathered reeds
(b) With right side facing, bugle beads backstitched across the reeds. Middle row, small beads on the tie stitch. Additional small beads added afterwards

Beads sewn to the front of reverse smocked fabric

Cable stitch is worked in close rows on the reverse side of the gathered fabric. This will prevent stretching on certain areas such as cuffs or dress yokes where a firmer foundation is needed. It is beaded or re-embroidered on the front. Modern baby dresses worked in the Philippines show this construction, with the front reeds of the yoke embroidered with a series of tiny bullion knots.

This method is also described by Diana Keay in her leaflet *New Ideas for Smocking*, written for the Embroiderers' Guild. She mentions an eighteenth-century baby bonnet which is in the Embroiderers' Guild Collection. This has little buttonhole loops worked across the reeds on the bonnet crown.

Beads combined with stitchery

The reverse-stitched reeds make an excellent foundation for the addition of beadwork. The beads could be alternated with the bullion knots or buttonhole bars. They combine equally well with stem or chain stitches worked in random curves across the reeded surface.

Beaded ribbon

In her leaflet, Diana Keay suggests the application of ribbon, sewn along the length with tiny beads, across the smocked reeds. Ruched ribbon could be applied, held by a bead at every fold.

Canadian or North American smocking

This is a different type of reverse smocking. A grid

79 Smocked 'miser' purse with tassel. Twisted bead cord handle, beaded machine lace edge worked on water-dissolvable fabric, beaded holding ring. (*Sue Golds, City and Guilds Embroidery, South Notts College of Further Education*)

of pattern dots is marked onto the wrong side of the fabric and a ruching stitch is formed by picking up the dots in pattern order.

It is often worked on velvet or heavy satins for use on cushions and soft furnishings; but many other types of fabric are suitable. On the right side a lattice of soft deep pleats is formed. Beads may be sewn within these pleats, or onto the intersections after the smocking is worked.

Smocking with beads alone

Another version is worked from the right side of the fabric by picking up the cloth at intervals, each time with a beaded stitch. The connecting thread is passed beneath the fabric.

Mark the fabric on the right side with marker

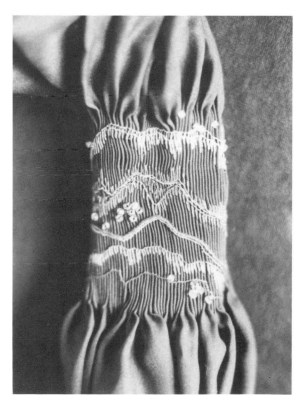

80 Smocked area of the purse, showing free smocking stitches across reverse smocked reeds with beads added afterwards. (*Sue Golds*)

82   Sample, smocking with beads, using the woven pattern as a guide. (*Janet Peacey*)

81   Bead-smocked, lace-edged pot-pourri pillow worked on satin, with the reeds held in triplets by the beads. (*Janet Peacey, member of the Smocking Group of the Embroiderers' Guild*)

Always work from left to right, staggering the rows to form a beaded honeycomb stitch.

A smock-gathering machine can be used to draw up the reeds. From the right side pick up the reeds three at a time and hold together with a beaded back stitch. Alternate the rows. The gathering threads are removed afterwards.

Beaded smocked quilting

Sue Rangeley uses this method to produce elaborate jackets, waistcoats and quilted bags. The top fabric, wadding and backing is first quilted together by machining parallel lines with metallic thread. These will form the reed ridges. The spacing will determine the depth of the reeds which are brought together at measured intervals to form a honeycomb smocking. Each stitch is sewn with a tiny bead. The metallic-thread machine-stitching now forms a diamond mesh pattern with a bead at each padded intersection.

Design ideas

Decorative or beaded smocking is suitable for use on many other articles in addition to the more traditional smocked garments. Evening bags and miser purses, herb sachets and pillows, cushions, caps and bonnets allow the use of smocking within their structure.

Working very freely

The smocking does not have to conform to a rigid reed formation. By altering the length and row distance of the gathering stitches, uneven folds or

pencil or iron-on smocking dots. Alternatively choose a striped, ridged or weave-patterned fabric.

Starting at the top left, fasten on at the first dot with a back stitch. Thread on a bead and pick up the next dot alongside to the right. Sew the two dots together by taking a double back stitch through both the bead and the cloth. Pass the needle behind the cloth and come up at the next dot alongside on the row below. Pick up the next dot to the right and make a beaded back stitch as before. Take the needle under the cloth and come up at the next dot alongside on the row above. Make a beaded back stitch with the next dot to the right.

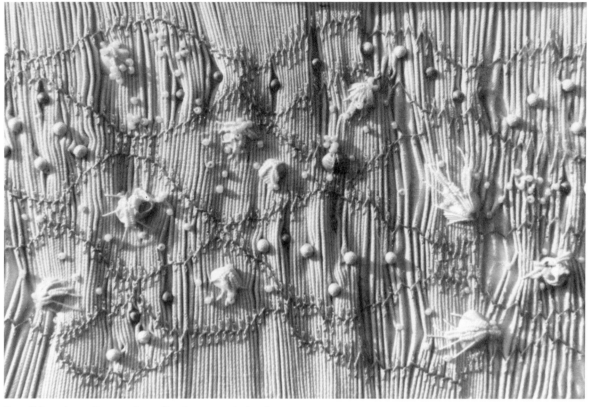

83 'Vacations Remembered'. Cretan stitch, free needleweaving over shells with added beads onto manipulated reverse smocked reeds. (*Julie M. Milne, teacher of English smocking from Glencoe, Illinois, USA*)

gathers are obtained. Manipulate these to suggest textures in embroidery such as bark, land or wave formation. Sew beads onto the distorted reed structure to emphasize parts of the design. Experimental embroidery and soft sculpture gain an added textural quality. The design is enhanced by allowing areas of light to contrast with patches of deep shade, brightened by the sparkle of hidden beads.

Ruching and shirring

Stitch fine, ruched fabric into position with beads or sequins. The ruching threads are drawn up first and beads worked along the lines of ruching, or the ruched fabric is held onto a backing tape by the stitched bead embroidery.

To suggest texture on embroidery, work the shirring very freely and hold down at intervals with tiny beads, or sew massed beads within the hollows.

Beaded quilting

Bedcovers and garments were originally quilted to give extra warmth. Various types of padding were used in different parts of the world, according to climate and availability. Until recent times sheep's wool and cotton batting were common forms of insulation. For hundreds of years, a silk wadding called *mawata* has given warmth to the people of China and Japan. This wadding is made from degummed silk cocoons which have been opened out and built up into layers on smooth bell-shaped moulds. It is available today. Modern synthetic waddings come in different weights, or thicknesses, and will wash and dry clean.

Beadwork was not added to quilting until it was used in a decorative context. The padded clothing of the Tudor and Elizabethan periods was embroidered with pearls and precious jewels. Later, during the eighteenth century, elaborate quilted petticoats were worn. The fashion for including beads on quilted embroidery would appear to be of more recent origin.

Although beads may be added to items or garments which are already quilted, it is far better to work out the design beforehand, with both the beads and quilting in mind.

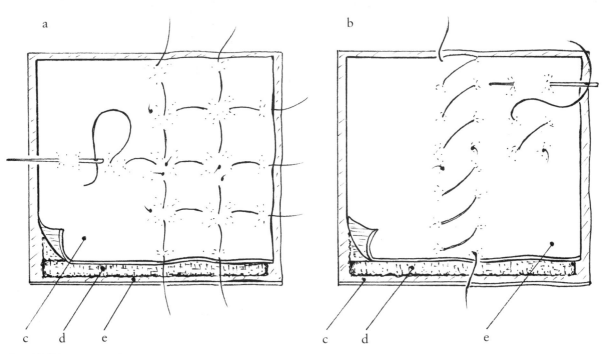

84 Quilting preparation
(a) Hand quilting: tacking through all three layers, working from the centre outwards, right side uppermost
(b) Machine quilting: tailor tacks, working from the centre, first upwards, then downwards, backing side uppermost
(c) Outer fabric
(d) Wadding
(e) Backing or lining fabric

Hand quilting methods

Flat quilting

Traditionally the two layers of fabric are sewn together with a running stitch, chain stitch or a back stitch. There is no padding between the layers. It gave added body to the bedcurtains and cover cloths in use during the sixteenth and seventeenth centuries.

English quilting

This is also called 'wadded quilting' as there is a layer of padding inserted between the top and bottom layers. The three layers of fabric – fine muslin backing, wadding and top fabric – are all tacked together beforehand.

Use a fine thread for tacking and tie a knot in the end. Always tack from the middle of the work outwards, making a grid pattern across the three layers with the lines approximately 5 cm (2 in.) apart. Start from the centre each time and do not

85 'Seed Head'. Trapunto quilting with beads, bugles and stitchery. Design based on a Cleome plant of the Caper family, Africa. (*Barbara Collins*)

86 Machine quilted sample. Freely embroidered whipped stitch sections worked first in shaded thread; satin stitch quilting worked under the foot, beads added afterwards. (*Jane Davies*)

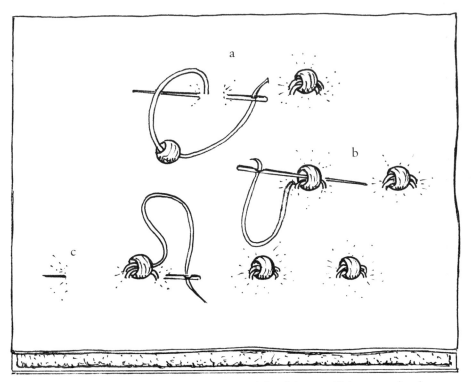

87   Method for quilting with beads alone
(a) Fasten on with a back stitch. Pick up a bead and make
 a back stitch through all three layers
(b) Pass the needle back through the bead
(c) Take a back stitch through all layers and come up in
 position for the next bead

fasten off the threads, but leave the ends hanging
free. When the work is finished, remove these
tacking threads by pulling on the knotted ends.
Once again, traditional stitches are running stitch
and back stitch.

Trapunto or raised quilting
The quilting design is worked in running or back
stitch onto two layers of unpadded fabric. For the
best results, use a quilting mull or muslin for the
backing. Afterwards, padding is inserted into certain design areas from the wrong side by slitting or
parting the muslin threads in the backing fabric.
These may be sewn up again afterwards if
necessary.

Italian or corded quilting
Designs are worked on two layers of fabric and are
outlined with parallel lines of running stitch, like
tramlines. A soft quilting yarn, called quilting wool,
is threaded into a large-eyed tapestry needle and run
between the tramlines from the back of the work. It
is necessary to come out and go back into the work
for each stitch. Remember to allow extra to go
round the corners.

Machine quilting methods
With the presser foot on
Some machines are provided with a quilting foot
which has a shorter turned-up front to make it
easier to sew over thick wadding. Several have a
small guide, which slots into the rear of the foot and
aids the sewing of straight rows.

Most people are familiar with straight-stitched
machine quilting; but many other stitches work just
as well. Try using zigzag stitch for a change. Do not
be tempted to close the stitch length up to a fine satin
stitch or the fabric will jam under the machine.
Choose any of the more open type of automatic
stitches or some of those called utility stitches which
are used for blind-hemming or overlocking. Be
prepared to experiment; these stitches combine well
with the addition of beads which are sewn on
afterwards.

Twin needles
A double stitch line appears on the front of the
work, a single thread zigzag on the reverse. Sew a
series of parallel straight lines or work a crossways
grid. Machine wavy twin-needle lines, then turn the
fabric and sew wavy lines the other way. Sew beads
to the intersections of the lines, or along the double
lines.

Detached petals or leaves
Mark the outline of a leaf or flower petal onto the
prepared quilting fabric. Machine this outline with

a straight stitch. Cut out the shape and oversew with satin stitch to cover both the edges and the outline. If the fabric is very fine, satin stitch first and then cut out as close to the stitches as possible without snagging them. Apply a beaded centre to a completed flower. Stitch beads to outline leaf veins, or fill in pattern areas with tiny beads.

Free machine quilting
A darning foot allows the worker to sew free machine embroidery without the need to stretch the work in an embroidery frame. This is ideal for free machine quilting. The feed teeth should be lowered or covered with a cover plate.

Tacking　To prevent the machine foot from snagging, tack the fabric layers together with tailor-tack stitches on the wrong side of the work. The stitch is formed by taking short horizontal scoops through the fabric layers with the tacking-thread needle. Work rows up the fabric, starting from the centre as before. Rows of tiny horizontal stitches appear on the right side of the work.

Sewing the beads

Beads sewn spaced out
The beading thread should tone in with the fabric background colour. Fasten on with a knot on the wrong side of the work. Run the needle through the layers of wadding and come out in position for the first bead. Make a back stitch, pick up a bead and sew with another back stitch. Run the needle through the layers and come out ready to sew the next bead, repeating the back stitches.

Beads sewn close together
Quilting stitches worked close together flatten the padding. These flat areas make a firm base for close-packed beading. Beads and bugles, crystals and sequins of all kinds are sewn down in the normal manner with added back stitches for security.

Any of the other bead sewing methods can be applied to beadwork on quilting. Sew beads and sequins with other beads, stand bugle beads on end, overlap sequins. Lay little strings of beads over the padded parts of the quilting, or combine with free needleweaving stitchery.

Quilting with beads alone

Beads can be used as part of the actual quilting process. This is only possible on hand-stitched work and is a version of tie-quilting.

Method
Prepare the layers of fabric by tacking them

together. The beads are sewn a distance apart, according to the chosen pattern or design. This may take the form of a grid or it may be based on free design.

It is necessary to mark the positions of the bead ties beforehand. A small dot marked with a hard pencil is the easiest way. The dot will be covered by the bead. Use a sharpened dressmakers' crayon in white on darker fabrics. Do not be tempted to use a

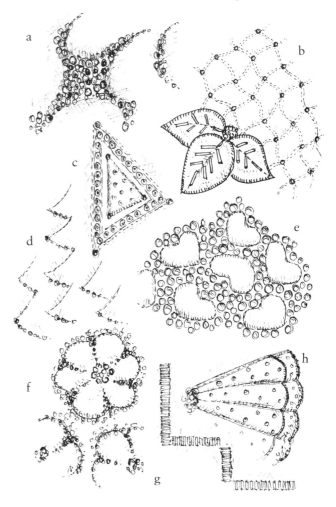

88　Design ideas for beaded quilting
(a) Beads in the hollows of padded quilting
(b) Twin-needle machine lines with beads at intersections. Detached leaves with bugle bead leaf veins
(c) Machined quilted outlines with beads added
(d) Zigzag machine lines with beads added
(e) White china beads surrounding trapunto padded shapes
(f) Beads sewn to form flower petal shapes
(g) Quilting with bugle bead lines
(h) Fan shape in hand or machine quilting with beads added to the surface

water-dissolvable marker as it is not advisable to dampen under the beads.

Fasten on with a knot and a back stitch. Run the sewing thread through the wadding layers and come up in the position for the first bead. Take a back stitch, sew the bead in place with a second back stitch. Pass the needle through all layers, to the wrong side, keeping close to the bead. Make a back stitch on the wrong side in the same place. Lay the thread across the back of the work, and come out ready for the next beaded tie-stitch. Make a back stitch, but do not pull the connecting thread tight; leave it slack. Failure to do this will distort the quilted fabric.

Design ideas and application

The undulating nature of the quilted fabric provides hollows and crevices where beading can be applied. Do not get carried away and sew beads into every available nook and cranny. The sparkle of beads and sequins naturally draws the eye to certain sections of the design. These areas need to be well-planned beforehand. Drop a few loose beads and let them roll into the hollows. Take away or add more beads until the balance is correct. Then sew down the beads.

Beads are excellent for outlining important design features. Vary the size of the beads or sequins. Save the larger, more important ones for the focal point of the design and gradually decrease the size towards the outer edges.

Beads and sequins may be added to already printed or dyed fabrics. At one time different types of fabric craft or embroidery were kept apart. Today's textile workers enjoy the interplay of mixed media. Fabric painting and printing is given dimension by the quilted outline. The prudent addition of beadwork will enliven the work.

Quilted bead-decorated fabric can be made up into padded garments, bags, teacosies, cushions, panels and wallhangings.

8 | Beaded edges, fringes, tassels and cords

Many of the different cultural and historical bead stringing methods are adaptable for use in modern embroidery. It is possible to combine these various types of stringing and looping for fringes and tassels. They make an excellent finish on hems and edges or can form an integral part of the design in fashion garments and accessories.

Bead stringing methods

Threads

String the beads with synthetic threads, such as Polytwist, polyester, or Drima. Silk was used in the past. Whichever one you choose, wax it first for added strength. The other alternative is monofilament nylon or fishing line. This strong but very fine and virtually transparent thread, should not be waxed. It can be used double.

Needles

Work with a long beading needle, in as fine a size as it is possible to pass the working thread through the needle eye. If you are working with mixed beads the smallest hole is the optimum size.

Single strings

Various types and shapes of beads are suitable for threading. Beads of a similar shape and size are strung to make the individual strands of fringes or tassels or for use on their own. The beads may be rocaille or bugle, cut crystal or clay – the choice depends on the article onto which they are sewn. The design impact relies on the effect of strands of similar massed beads, with the added element of motion when they are attached to clothing.

Mixed beads, providing they go well together, are far more decorative when used for single strings or for a series of single strings set at spaced intervals, than for massed fringing.

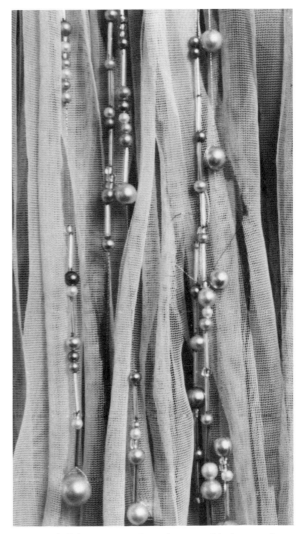

89 Beaded hanging. Soft sculpture with long nylon-filament fabric strips and hanging pearls with bugle beads. (*Barbara Capewell, City and Guilds Embroidery*)

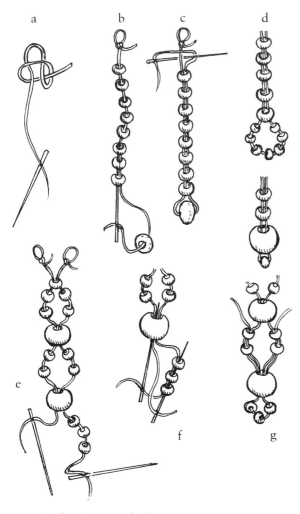

91 Fringed epaulette worked in a variety of closely packed beads, bugles, gemstones and sequins. (*Joyce Law, Embroiderers' Guild Collection*)

90 Bead stringing methods
(a) Making the slip knot
(b) Taking the needle back through the threaded beads
(c) Buttonhole fastening stitch round the thread
(d) Different bead string ends
(e) Double string using two needles
(f) Finishing by passing both needles through the end beads
(g) Both threads taken up ready for tying off

Making separate strings

Take more thread than you think you will need. It is doubled back on itself during the working process and ends should be left for attaching the beaded string afterwards. Start by tying a slip knot near the thread end. This is done by forming a loop and then taking the thread end over and round this loop and back through the new loop formed. This knot will prevent the first bead from slipping off. It can be tightened or released afterwards.

Thread on as many beads as you wish for the length of the string. Take the thread through the one end bead and then pass the needle back up through all the beads, coming out at the first bead again. Hold the beads down firmly in position and make a half hitch or buttonhole stitch over and round both threads, using the needle.

An alternative method is to work these single strings in position onto the embroidery. Fasten the thread on firmly with a knot and two back stitches. Thread the beads as explained for the separate strings, bring the needle back through the beads and make a half hitch as before but finish off with two more back stitches into the starting position.

Decorative string ends

Variations can be made in the number or type of bead threaded at the string end before the needle is passed back up through the beads. An odd number of little beads will form a tiny loop. Leave three or five before threading back up. Thread on a large end bead, pass the needle through one, three or five small beads, back through the large bead and up again. There are many permutations on this theme.

92 Beaded fringe on the epaulette. (*Joyce Law*)

Double strings

Separate bead strings, worked on two needles, are threaded and joined at intervals, with both threads going through a larger or more decorative central bead. Thread two needles, each with a separate thread, and tie a slip knot in each thread end. Pass the two needles through a single bead. Divide and thread an equal number of smaller beads onto each string. Pass both needles through a larger bead and divide again. Repeat as necessary.

It is usual to end with a large bead. Take both threads out through the large bead, pass the first needle through one or more small beads and let it hang. Take the second needle and pass through these small beads the opposite way. Take both threads back through the large bead. For short strings thread back right up to the top. For long strings, thread up through several beads on each string, come over and back through these beads until you reach the large bottom bead. Tie off firmly above this bead.

Joining by the use of one needle

A single string of beads can be looped back onto itself at intervals to make little rings. These rings form the basis of a variety of patterns, depending on the order of threading. Little flower necklaces are made in this manner and the same method is the basic structure for net or trellis work.

More complicated patterns are achieved with the use of two needles. For more information consult Anne E. Gill's book, *Beadwork – The Technique of Stringing, Threading and Weaving*.

Knotted bead strings

The beads are knotted into a string of double thread during the working process. Make a slip knot at one end of the thread and pass a bead down to the bottom. Make a loose overhand knot below the bead. Do not pull this tight. Slide a heavy needle into the loose knot, and gradually work the knot up to lie close beneath the bead. Take out the needle and tighten the knot. Repeat the process.

A modern fashion application is the knotting of beads within the fine fabric of evening wear. The beads may be knotted at intervals within fabric strips, or onto the ends of fine layers of handkerchief points.

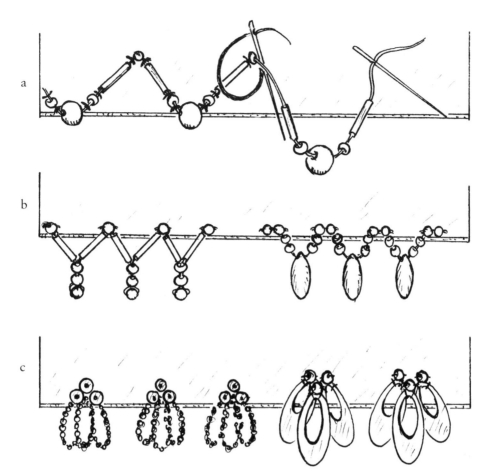

93 Edges
(a) Strung beads and bugles couched to a fabric edge with a second thread
(b) Beads strung and attached at intervals with the working thread
(c) Bead loops and sequins sewn to the fabric edge

Edges

Some of the methods described above are used for making decorative edges which are worked onto hems or the bases of banners, bags or fashion accessories.

Strung edges

String a repeat pattern sequence of various bead types as long as the finished edge. Fasten on at one end and couch into position using a second thread. Push the beads up evenly and stitch between every two or three beads. Fasten off firmly.

Strung loops

The thread is fastened into the base or hem at one end. Little loops or points of beads are threaded and secured at regular intervals spaced out along the hem. The type and patterning of these beads can be altered. A combination of long bugle, rocaille, long bugle will give a pointed, triangular shape. Experiment with a random selection of shapes and sizes for inclusion on free embroidery.

Bead loops need not be confined to the edges and hems of garments. Little loops of beads or beads and bugles are used to decorate the fabric surface, as an addition to embroidered beading, or on their own.

A study of Victorian bead-edged purses will give the embroiderer many ideas for interpretation. Favourite edgings are formed of bead loops twisted round each other in a variety of ways.

Fringes

How to thread – commercial method

While the needle-threaded method of making bead strings for applying as fringes gives scope for the

inclusion of different types of beads, it can be time-consuming. It is much quicker to make plain fringing from strings of commercially threaded beads.

Take a string of threaded beads. Knot the end of this string to your working thread, which should be at least three times as long as the planned fringe. Slip one bead down over the knot until it reaches halfway on the working thread. Tie a knot round it.

Take the loose end of the working thread back up and tie it to the other end, below the knot which secures the bead string. You should now have a double thread tied to the bead string. Slide the correct number of beads from the string, over both knots, and down the double thread to rest on the tied bottom bead. Leaving some spare thread, cut from the bead string and repeat the process for the next fringe piece. Each string takes only a few seconds to complete.

To secure the fringe pieces, sew each one individually to a backing or tape and tie off in pairs before cutting the ends. This tape can then be

95 Method for fringe strings
(a) Tie bead string to the fringe thread
(b) Pass bottom bead over the knot, and tie at halfway position
(c) Loop up thread end and tie back onto fringe thread
(d) Pass required number of beads over both knots down onto the fringe thread. Cut off

a	b	c	d

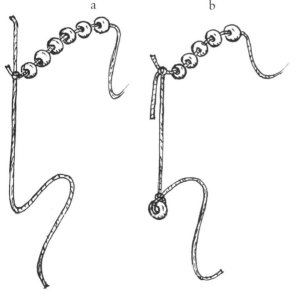
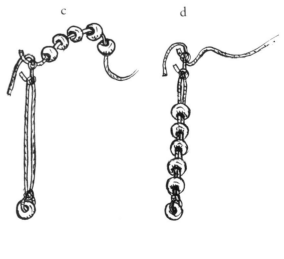

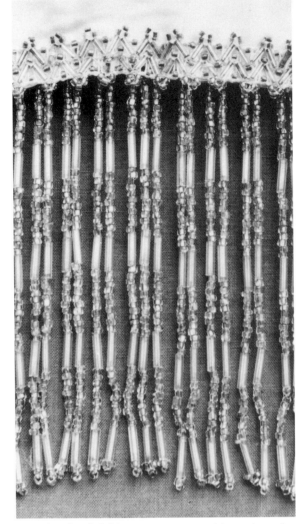

96 Silver-beaded fringe on a 1920s white satin stole. (*Author's collection*)

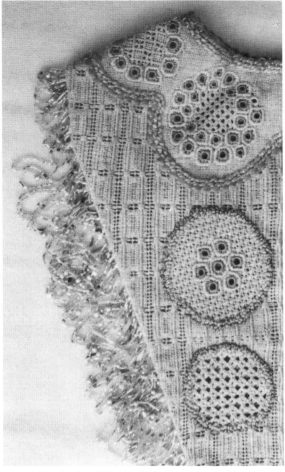

97 Fringed tabard. Looped fringing of varied beads and bugles on the side edge of a drawn fabric tabard. (*Nancy Evans*)

applied. Alternatively, work directly into the hem or working fabric.

Trellis-work fringes

It is possible to use some of the stringing and joining methods already described to make other types of meshed fringes and decorative edges.

Worked up and down
Thread a string of beads and loop back into a small circle by re-threading into one of the beads. Continue threading beads and join to the original string at regular intervals. This will give a continuous figure-of-eight pattern. Make a similar string of beads, this time joining onto the first pair at the

same intervals. This will build up a diamond trellis pattern.

Worked horizontally
Here, bead loops are worked across the row, and fastened onto the hem or base at intervals. A second row of bead loops is worked into the first, joining at mid-loop. This forms a looped mesh.

Tassels

Making straight tassels

One of the simplest methods is to make a fringe with all the top ends secured onto a tape. Place a folded cord, loop or other fastening onto one end of the tape. Roll up the tape enclosing the ends of the

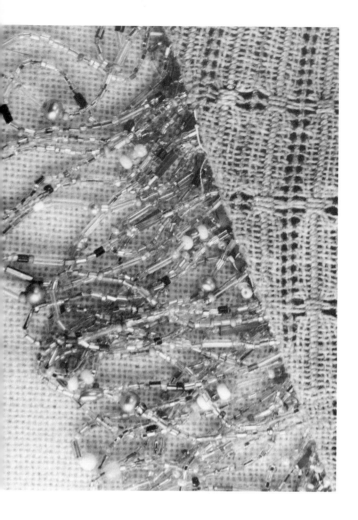

98 Detail of tabard fringe. Fabric is fine, woven Welsh wool. (*Nancy Evans*)

fastening loop. Secure firmly by sewing through from back to front several times. The top of this roll of fringed tape can now be padded and bound with thread to keep it in position. When the padding is finished, cover it with little strings of beads, sewn vertically and later couched into position. Alternatively, sew beads singly to cover the padding completely.

Looped tassels

A looped fringe is sewn onto the tape and rolled up in a similar manner. Alternatively, sew the tassel loops into a folded cord end.

Beads with ribbon and braids

Sew beads to hold folded, ruched or pleated ribbon in place. Alternatively a beadwork design is sewn onto the ribbon or braid before applying to the fabric. Another method is to wind strips of beaded ribbon round firmer braid or strips of leather. Narrow ribbon can be threaded through large-holed beads and knotted above and below.

Doreen Williamson has added tiny beads to the ribbon loops of rugfork trimming. The ribbon is

99 Method for tassels
(a) Secure beaded fringe threads to tape
(b) Roll up tape to enclose cord loop. Stitch tape end
(c) Pad the top and bind with thread
(d) Sew bead strings to the padding

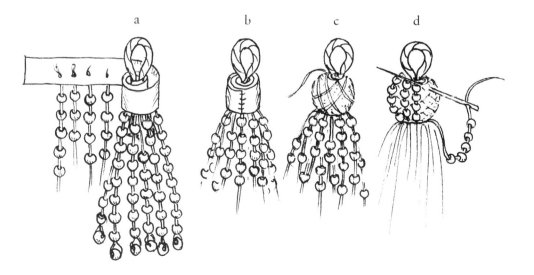

a   b   c   d

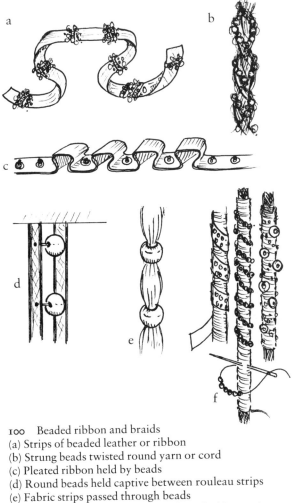

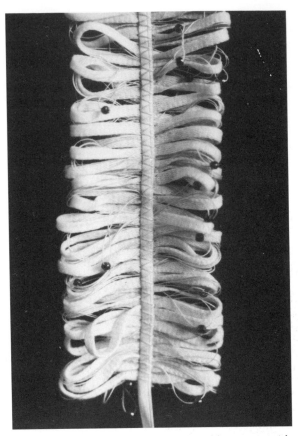

100   Beaded ribbon and braids
(a) Strips of beaded leather or ribbon
(b) Strung beads twisted round yarn or cord
(c) Pleated ribbon held by beads
(d) Round beads held captive between rouleau strips
(e) Fabric strips passed through beads
(f) Wrapped cords with added beads and ribbon strip

101   Sample of rugfork trimming. Ribbon tape with small beads on fine threads. (*Doreen Williamson, South Notts College of Further Education*)

wound round the prongs of the rugfork and held together by straight-stitch machining down the centre. More ribbon is wound on as the braid is pushed through the sewing machine. A similar tool, called a weaver's reed, allows a one-sided braid to be sewn with larger loops on one edge.

Beads with rouleau

Sew beads onto rouleau strips and loops, either down the middle or to one side. If you have large-holed beads, pass the rouleau through the beads and tie at intervals with overhand knots. Join parallel rouleau strips at intervals with a large bead held captive in between.

Beaded cords

It is possible to work beads in with the elements of

cords or plaits by passing them onto the working thread beforehand. If this is too thick, incorporate the beads by first stringing onto a finer thread and working this in with the thicker one. Another method is to sew the beads on separately afterwards. The entire cord can be beaded by sewing little strings of beads around and through, close packed or spaced out. Couch a thick cord onto the fabric at intervals, allowing loops to hang freely. Twist beads round these loops, or cover the couched area with strings of tiny beads as a form of raised padding.

Wrapped and coiled thread

Incorporate beads in wrapped thread work by stringing the beads onto the wrapping thread beforehand or sew beads onto the wrapping itself.

Working freely

Much more freedom of expression is possible in this

type of work which is suitable for inclusion on banners, wallhangings and panels, three-dimensional work, and soft sculpture. Any of the methods described above is suitable for working freely. Most of the methods for sewing and stringing beads have already been discovered; it is up to the worker to make a personal interpretation.

Mave Buckroyd has incorporated beads with ribbon and thread loops and machine-sewn lace-work or water-dissolvable fabric to make an exotic headdress, the design elements based on seaweed.

Beads may be incorporated so that they become part of the construction. Beads are worked in with the stitchery, threaded over or woven in. To take away the beads would leave the design incomplete. It is a satisfying way of working.

102 'Seaweed Head'. Machine embroidery on water-dissolvable fabric with strings of beads intertwined. (*Mave Buckroyd, City and Guilds Embroidery, South Notts College of Further Education*)

9 Tambour beading

Chain stitch embroidery, formed with the tambour hook, was not used to secure beadwork until the late nineteenth century. The inspiration of Louis Ferry, a workshop manager from Lunéville near Strasbourg, it became known in England as Lunéville work. The method is in use today for beading on fashion garments, *haute couture* work, and theatrical and entertainment costume. Once mastered, it is a quick and versatile method. Round beads, sequins of different types and bugle beads of varying lengths are all suitable, the size depending on background fabric, size of hook and the type of thread used.

The origins of tambour work

The use of a hook to work chain stitches through fabric is said to have originated in China. Chain stitch embroidery has been worked in India for centuries. In Kutch embroidery, the chain stitching is combined with mirror-work and was equally popular in Sind and Baluchistan. Nineteenth-century Indo-Portuguese embroidery from Goa featured chain stitching in metal threads.

The tamboured chain stitch is found throughout the Asian subcontinent, and in Iran and Turkey was worked from the late seventeenth century onwards. It is possible that chain stitch embroidery, worked with a hook, was introduced to Europe and thence to England even as early as the fifteenth century. Sylvia Groves, in her *History of Needlework Tools* (David & Charles, 1973), records the use of the word 'crochet' in the wardrobe accounts of Edward IV. Free crochet, or *crochet en air*, was a later development.

By the late eighteenth century the work was called 'tambouring', after the drum-shaped frame which originally came from the East. The tambour work was not only a speedier method suitable for the embroidery workshop, it was also considered an elegant occupation for the aristocratic lady which allowed her delicate hands to be seen to advantage.

103 Seed beads. Tambour beaded collar, first quarter of the twentieth century. (*Author's collection*)

The fine muslins manufactured during the late eighteenth century were a suitable background for the linear chain-stitched embroidery. The advent of machine-made net in the early nineteenth century led to the development of chain-stitched Limerick lace and it was later incorporated into other whitework embroidery. The addition of beads to the chain stitching came at a period during the late nineteenth century when heavily beaded clothing and trimmings were highly fashionable.

Many of these trimmings were made by out-workers in their own homes, while the tambour beaders in the workrooms were the victims of the sweated labour system and worked in miserable conditions for a bare subsistence wage. Joan Edwards in her small book, *The Bead Embroidered Dress*, records that the problems of the workers were as bad in America as in Europe, and workers who emigrated to Australia or New Zealand fared little better.

The art of tambour beading reached its peak during the 1920s when it was featured on evening dresses. At times, not only was the entire dress surface covered, but free-hanging tasselled skirts gave added weight to an already heavy garment.

Tambour beading is once again used in contemporary fashion. Beads and sequins are lighter and the general effect is more fluid.

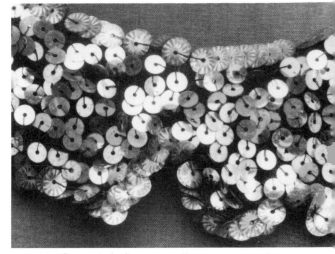

105 Tambour-stitched sequin collar, 1930s. (*Author's collection*)

---

104 Tambour beading hooks
From the top Two hooks given to Daphne Troughton by a Mrs Hawkes, who worked as a tambour beader over 60 years ago; a 40-year-old hook, a 20-year-old hook and a modern hook belonging to and used by Daphne Troughton of Ells and Farrier Ltd.

Tambour frames

The original circular wooden tambour frame was supported below by two horseshoe-shaped wooden hoops set at right-angles to one another and fastened in the middle. This gave the worker free access beneath the embroidery which was stretched

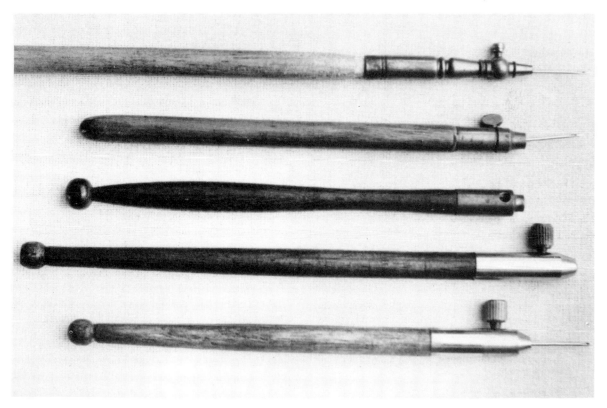

across the top of the frame and held in place by a leather strap. Much of the commercial embroidery from the Middle East was worked by men. They would sit cross-legged on the ground with the tambour frame supported between the knees. The Europeans favoured the rectangular wooden frame, held at either side by two uprights, or a circular frame held by one upright.

Many ethnic societies, like the Peruvian Indians on the shores of Lake Titicaca, work coarse chain stitch embroidery freely in the hand. It is essential that any fine work, especially tambour beading, should be worked on well-stretched fabric in a free-standing frame.

Circular frames should be free-standing with the inner ring bound to prevent the fabric from slipping. They are only suitable for working smaller motifs.

Framing the fabric

If the background fabric is fine, use the following method to frame the fabric:
1. Mount on top of already stretched calico or cotton, by pinning or tacking in place, and then cut away the calico from behind.
2. Reinforce the sides of the fabric with a stronger fabric. Sew to the top and bottom of the frame in the usual manner. Lace to the frame sides by lapping flat tape round the sides at intervals and hold it onto the reinforced fabric edge by pinning securely on each tape fold.

It is absolutely essential that the framed fabric should be quite taut. Any excess fabric is wound onto the upper round crosspiece of the frame and moved down as the work progresses.

Marking out the design

The beads are worked onto the underside of the fabric so the right side will face downwards. The design lines can be marked onto the reverse of the fabric, either with a medium-hard pencil or dress marker crayon. Remember that any asymmetrical pattern will come out mirror-imaged. Net embroidery is worked over a pattern placed below the work.

Hooks and needles

The tambour hook is formed of a holder or handle and the hook or needle. The needle is held in place with a horizontally placed thumbscrew. Some of the beautiful old hooks had a screw-off cap at one end into which spare needles could be inserted.

The needles have a tiny sharp hook on one end and are made from the needles used for the Cornely

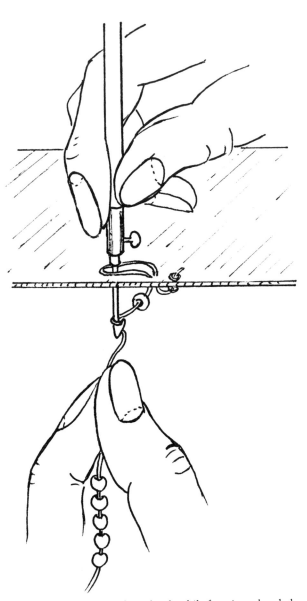

106   Holding the tambour hook while forming a beaded chain stitch.

chain stitch trade machine. The top, flattened end is cut off and they are available in four sizes. The two finer sizes are for use with delicate fabrics. The medium size is used to apply embroidery silk and 60-denier cotton. The very coarse hook can be used for applying thin wools or thicker threads.

Insert the needle into the handle so that the open end of the hook always faces the same way as the screw. This acts as a guide as the stitch is made with the screw facing in whichever direction you are going.

Threads

It is essential that the thread should be on a reel or spool which is placed on a reel-holder to the left of the frame for right-handed workers. Alternatively place the spool onto a knitting needle or metal rod slotted into the left side of the frame. The thread should run freely and not snag.

To sew small beads and sequins, 60-denier cotton is used, either in a colour to tone with the background fabric, or with the beads. For contrast, a fine metallic thread can be worked, either with the beads or as separate decoration. Experiment with different threads – some synthetics may split and fray, others behave well.

Beads and sequins

These are best purchased ready strung. If the beads are loose, string them first. The right, shiny side of sequins, and the inner side of cup sequins, should face downwards so that they come out the right way up when sewn in place.

Methods of work

Do not attempt to sew on any beads until you have mastered the basic stitches and can move the hook easily in any direction you wish.

Some people prefer to start by working on net, so that they can see the hook and the working thread beneath. Others are put off by this and prefer to guide the thread from beneath by feel. A good compromise is a semi-opaque fabric; but whichever you use, practice will make the stitch formation completely automatic. Reverse all the following instructions if you are left-handed.

Fastening on

Hold the end of the spool thread beneath the fabric between the first finger and the thumb of the left hand. For extra tension first wind the thread between the last two fingers as if working free crochet.

Insert the needle into the cloth keeping the tambour hook upright and with the screw facing away from you. From beneath, lay the thread over the hook. Keeping a slight tension raise the hook. At the same time twist round anticlockwise keeping the hook in an upright position. A loop is drawn through. The twist stops the loop from falling out of the hook, and also prevents the hook from catching in the cloth. It helps to press lightly backwards with the needle shaft as the hooked end comes out of the

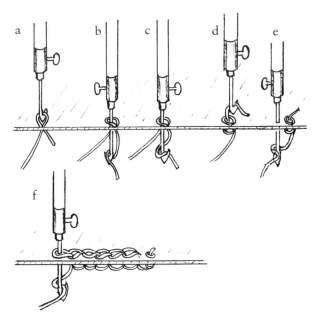

107 Method for fastening on
(a) Lay the bottom thread over the hook and draw a loop through the cloth
(b), (c) and (d) Turn the hook and draw the free end of the thread up through the loop first formed
(e) Tighten the end into a knot. Turn the hook and lay the bottom thread over the hook. Turn the hook and draw loop to the surface
(f) Turn the hook the opposite way and draw another loop through the first one. Repeat to make chain stitch on the surface

cloth. It should go in and out with a definite 'ping'.

With the hook facing forward, insert into the same place and draw the free thread end through the first loop to the surface. Pull this free end tight. For greater security, work a second small stitch to the left and a third one back in the first hole. To make a chain stitch insert the hook, facing away from you, a short distance away and draw up another chain loop. Each chain stitch is formed in this manner. Do not hold the thread beneath too tightly or it will not be possible to pull the following loop through. Both the length and the direction of the chain stitches can be varied. When zigzag chain is worked, the direction is changed on every stitch.

Finishing off

Make the final chain slightly longer, then pull the previous chain stitch up onto the hook through this last stitch. Pull on the bottom thread to tighten into a knot. Make the next chain stitch in the same place, through the cloth. Pull the previous chain through and tighten. Pull a final loop through to the top and cut off.

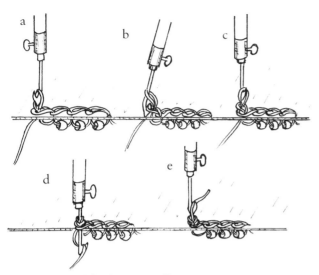

108 Method for fastening off
(a) Make a longer chain stitch
(b) Slip the needle shaft down through this chain and pick up the previous chain with the hook
(c) Draw this chain through the first long chain, and pull the underneath thread to tighten the knot
(d) Make a stitch in the same place, through the cloth and draw up a longer chain. Pull the previous chain through again and tighten the bottom thread
(e) Bring a final chain to the surface, cut the loop and pull the thread end down

The draw-back stitch

After fastening on, a longer chain stitch is worked in an upright direction. As the hook is withdrawn, instead of keeping the tension on both sides of the work even, tighten the bottom thread and allow the top chain to slide back so that the loop on the hook is back at the starting point. Make a small chain stitch, going once again into the starting position to lock the stitch. Make a short chain stitch to the right, horizontal to the first upright stitch. Repeat the process. The result looks not unlike a button-hole stitch and can be used for edgings as well as for attaching beads and sequins. Work this stitch in circles for flowers or in semicircles for alternating fan stitch.

Working with beads and bugles

It is necessary to transfer the strung beads to the working thread. Tie the free end of the bead thread loosely into a slip knot and pass the working thread end through this knot. Tighten the slip knot securely and then pass the beads over the knot and down onto the working thread a few at a time. It is advisable to hold the work over a tray in case the thread should break during this operation. Sequins are transferred in a similar manner.

The beads are pushed up close to the cloth from

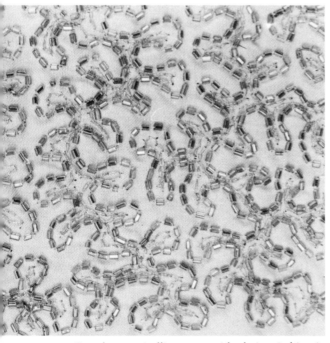

109   Sample, vermicelli pattern with chain stitching in gold metallic thread. (*Janet Lee White, City and Guilds course work, London College of Fashion*)

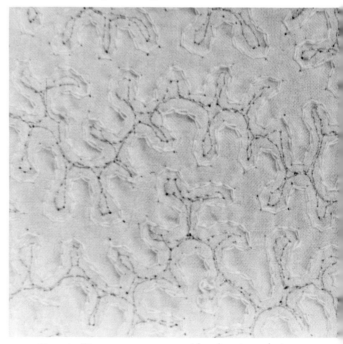

110   Vermicelli pattern, reverse side showing chain stitchery. (*Janet Lee White*)

111 Method for tambouring with beads
(a) Take a string of threaded beads and make a loose overhand knot in the thread end. Slip the reel thread end through the knot loop
(b) Tighten the knot and slip the beads down onto the reel thread
(c) Push up a bead with the left finger and thumb and hold close to the underside of the cloth while the chain stitch is made

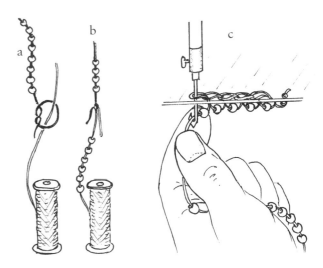

below, one at a time. The chain stitch is formed from the thread between each bead. The stitches should be made the length of the bead or bugle to allow the beads to lie flat. Hold each bead between the first finger and thumb and hold up as the stitch is formed. A number of beads can be held ready for immediate use in the remaining fingers of the left hand.

When groups of beads are sewn the chain stitch should be the length of the bead group. If you wish the group of beads to stand up, or to hang down in loops, shorten the length of the chain stitch accordingly.

Groups of beads or single bugle beads can be sewn using the zigzag chain. It is advisable to make a single small chain at the end of each beaded zigzag to secure the beads.

The draw-back stitch is used to sew down lines of bugles or rows of bead groups. Mark parallel guide lines on the cloth. Fasten on. Push up the beads into position as the upright stitch is being drawn back and fix at the bottom with the small chain stitch.

Make the stitch to the right the width of the bead or bugle to allow them to lie flat side by side.

Working with sequins

Transfer the strung sequins to the working thread, face downwards. Sequins with a hole in the middle are sewn down with a chain stitch that is only half

112 Tambour beading following the outline of discharge printing on cotton lawn. Single line stitching and broader bands of bead triplets. (*Jane Dew*)

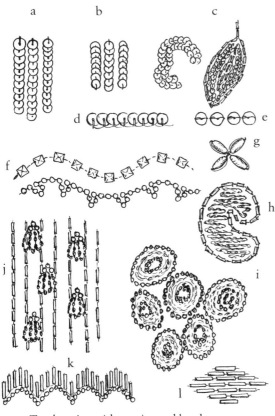

113 Tambouring with sequins and beads
(a) Lapped sequins facing downwards
(b) Lapped sequins facing opposite ways
(c) Lapped sequins to outline or fill in a shape
(d) Sequins held with the draw-back stitch
(e) Sequins stitched twice into the centre hole
(f) Border of square beads and vermicelli trail
(g) Pearls sewn singly into a cluster
(h) Bugle bead outline, tambour chain infill
(i) Cut-bead outlines with infill of tamboured metallic thread
(j) Bugle lines with looped clusters
(k) Draw-back stitched bugles with round beads
(l) Bugles stitched in rows, alternating spaces

the width of the sequin so that they overlap one another, each sequin covering the centre hole of the one before. These are referred to as 'scaled sequins' and should overlap downwards when worked in vertical lines on garments.

Lapped sequins sewn in circles or spirals look very decorative as they catch the light at different angles. Sequins are made to stand up by placing each one between a design of already sewn spaced beads.

Sequins can be sewn down using the zigzag chain, or may be included in the upright of the draw-back

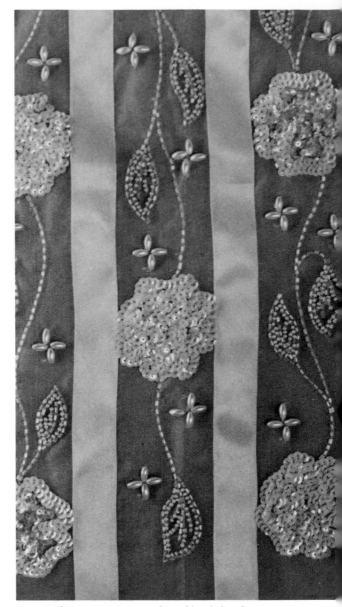

114 Iridescent sequins, pearls and bugle beads tamboured onto fine silk organza, between strips of applied satin ribbon. (*Daphne Randall, City and Guilds, London College of Fashion*)

stitch. After the first sequin is in place, the horizontal part of the draw-back stitch is worked the width of the sequin apart. This allows them to overlap just under halfway.

Sequins sewn down flat

First fasten on with a chain stitch. Make a stitch half the width of the sequin and draw back the stitch. Push up the sequin. Make another chain stitch into the same place as the starting chain to lock the sequin in place. Work the next stitch into the centre of the sequin and the following stitch out to the opposite edge. Repeat this sequence for each sequin.

Irregularly shaped sequins

These may be sewn down flat separately or overlapped according to the desired effect. Pendant shapes are added afterwards when the main bead-work is complete.

Using pearls and other beads

Beads need not necessarily be regular in shape. Variation is given to the work by altering the size of the beads and sequins and the density in which they are sewn. Direction plays an important part in design, not only when sewing sequins but also in the use of faceted beads and bugle beads.

Fringes and edgings

The technique used for making little loops of beads on the surface of the cloth can be applied to looped fringes. Mark off double the required fringe length on a template guide. Fasten on with small chain stitches. Push up the number of beads to equal the guide length. Bring the beaded loop back up to the cloth and make several small chain stitches, one bead-width away from the first stitch. This will form a looped fringe. Give variety by altering the spacing, or alternating different-colour loops.

Single stranded fringing

The bead thread is tied to the working thread in the usual manner. Slip one bead down onto the working thread, loop the thread end back up the finished length of the fringe plus 5 cm (2 in.). Tie this thread end back onto the working thread and pass the required length of beads down over the doubled thread. The end bead will keep them in place. Thread any odd number of beads to form the fringe end.

Different permutations of beads and bugles can form the fringe strand. These should be threaded in the correct order beforehand. Each separate fringe strand is sewn along a tape or directly to the fabric by pulling each thread end through with the hook, working several chain and pulling the final end through. Afterwards, tie off every two pairs of threads.

Edgings

Decorative edgings are worked onto the finished hemline, or on the fold line of a hem or facing before it is neatened. Vary a small, looped edged by sewing bugle, bead, bugle combinations. Add rows of droplets, or pendant sequins. Edges formed of combined bead types should be sewn as separate strings, each string restricted to one kind. They are then sewn so that they integrate with one another.

Working on net

Care should be exercised in the choice of bead size. Very small beads can slip through the net mesh. If the beading is at all spaced out it is advisable to back net with a fine fabric such as silk or organdie. When the beadwork is combined with tambour stitchery on net, work the stitchery from the right side of the net, then re-frame to work the beading from below.

Separate motifs are worked spaced out onto organdie or net. They are then cut out and applied to a fabric ground.

115 Tambour beading and quilting combined. Sample of fine, white organza with coloured padding inserted into the flower circles and between the beaded lines. (*Daphne Randall*)

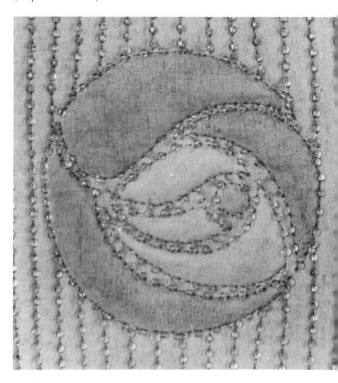

Designs and permutations

The best patterns are formed of continuous lines. This will limit the number of times it is necessary to fasten on and off. These linear designs can meander, scroll, cross over, or be worked in lines up and down the fabric. Border an area of sequins with a line of pearls or other beads. Separate and unify areas of different types of beading by outlining with chain stitch in gold thread.

A change of texture can be achieved by combining the beading with plain tambour chain stitching. Work the chain stitching first, from the right side, then add the beading with the wrong side uppermost.

Apply shapes, such as scattered leaves, flowers or butterflies, to the sequinned background. Cut the shapes from silk or velvet, hold down with chain stitch or draw-back stitch on the edges and re-embroider with spaced, single beads.

The placing of the design is important as bead embroidery of any type has great impact. Any garment which is entirely covered with beadwork needs larger areas that are non-reflective to contrast with the brighter highlights. This contrast should form an integral part of the design.

Fashion

Tambour beading is especially suitable for the decoration of evening wear and theatrical costume. Although much of the work is now done by machine, a place can always be found in the specialist market for individually designed and executed work.

116 Sequins sewn in vertical rows to the back of semi-transparent spotted voile. Applied velvet and stitchery. (*Paula Stypulkowski, Fashion Degree Course, Birmingham Polytechnic*)

117 Detail of sample. Long bugle beads massed together with small beads and sequins. Decorated with wrapped cords. (*Paula Stypulkowski*)

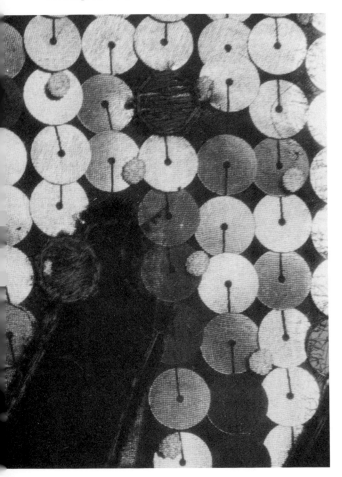

Paula Stypulkowski experimented with tambour beading on fine fabrics during her degree course at Birmingham Polytechnic. Her fashion work is designed to be worn in the evening, in artificial light. She has achieved subtle effects by tambouring bright sequins to the wrong side of fine fabric, and then adding softer colours on the right side. The underneath sequins glint through, even in a dim light.

Built-up layers of sequinned and beaded mesh are achieved by tambouring onto hot-water-dissolvable fabric. The fabric, which is a spun alginate, is dissolved by heating in water up to boiling point. Beads and sequins should be tested in boiling water beforehand. Most of the sequins obtained from reputable firms will stand up to this treatment.

It is essential that all the tambour stitches should interlock, or the beaded mesh will fall apart.

---

118 Experimental sample worked on organdie with tamboured beads and stitchery forming a netted mesh. (*Paula Stypulkowski*)

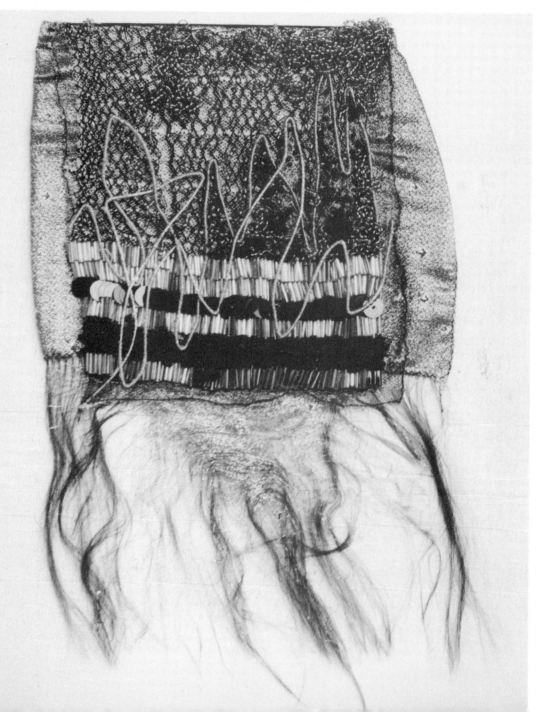

10 | *Making small beaded items*

Beadwork will enhance many small craft items provided that they are suited to the addition of raised decoration.

Pendants

Bead-embroidered pendants worked onto a fabric backing with bead-decorated edgings make excellent gifts. It is a good way of using any scraps of special fabric and assorted beads. The pendant may be round, oval, hexagonal, triangular or clamshell-shaped. Start with a circular pendant keeping the size as small as possible in relation to the fabric

119 Beaded pendants with shaped beads, pearls, round and cut beads, bugles and sequins. (*Angela Thompson*)

thickness. An oversize pendant looks clumsy.

Suitable fabric

Choose an unpatterned but slightly textured fabric in velvet, silks or synthetics. Line very fine fabric or mount onto iron-on interfacing. Cut the fabric piece large enough to place in the smallest-size ring frame. At last 2.5 cm (1 in.) is allowed beyond the pendant size for turnings.

Beads and thread

Select a variety of beads, sequins, bugles, pearls, crystals and drops in a toning colour scheme; or in one colour with gold or silver beads, sequins and jewellery findings. The larger, graded beads from broken necklaces make a good focal point to the design. Some stockists specialize in exotic beads and these may be purchased singly. Threads should match the background fabric.

Framing the work

Stretch a small fabric piece into a ring frame or dress a square frame with a cotton backing and sew several smaller separate pieces of the pendant fabric in position. These pieces can be cut out and the backing trimmed away after the beading is worked.

Making a card template

Mark a small circle in pencil onto thin card with a compass, or by drawing round an egg-cup. Cut out two card pieces for each pendant. Using one of these as a template guide, centre onto the framed fabric and tack round the outside edge. The pendant is worked within this marked shape.

Working the embroidery

Fasten on the thread securely with several back stitches in the centre of the circle. Take up the largest bead and sew in place. Arrange smaller beads around this focal point. Lay strings of smaller beads over and round these beads. Make radiating lines of bugle beads or sequins on the outer edges of the design area which should be well within your tacked shape. Any of the bead sewing methods described in Chapter 4 can be used.

Mounting on card

Cut the pendant shape at least 2.5 cm (1 in.) larger than the tacked outline. Snip at intervals from the outer edge of the fabric to the tacking line. Centre the worked piece over a card circle and overlap the slashed sections onto the reverse of the card. Glue each overlapped section in place with fabric adhesive onto the card back only, forming a covered circle. Cover the second card circle with a plain piece of the pendant fabric.

Finishing

The two card pieces are placed together with the right sides facing outwards. Oversew together with a beaded edge by taking up a bead onto each oversewing stitch. Leave a small space unsewn at the top to insert a fabric loop for the cord. This loop is made from a bias fabric strip cut twice the finished length plus seam allowances. Fold lengthways, machine up the seam line and turn as a rouleau to the right side. Press the seam to the back, fold over double and insert the ends into the top gap between the pendant cards. Finish sewing the edge, catching the loop in place. Thread with a cord or ribbon.

Pillows and pincushions

The size and type of pincushion depends on whether it is to be decorative or practical. In the past, elaborately beaded pincushions or 'pin-pillows' as they were sometimes called, were given as gifts to mark a special occasion – a wedding or the birth of a baby – or as a keepsake from a soldier or sailor on active service. The beads were not sewn on but applied with the aid of long pins.

The Mother's Day pincushion is first machine-embroidered on a satin background and then decorated in this manner. The heart shape needs to be well stuffed, preferably with a filling of bran as this will hold the pins well.

Make an inner case the same shape as the outer case. Leave a small hole at the top within the seam line. Insert the inner case through a larger opening in the outer case. Place a funnel into the inner case hole and then fill with bran which has been dried in

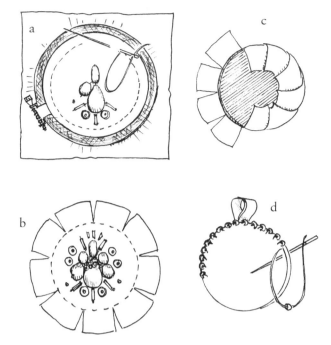

120 Beaded pendants
(a) Fabric stretched in a small ring frame, template circle outline tacked. Bead embroidery started
(b) Beading completed. Fabric trimmed and slashed to inner circle tacking line
(c) Fabric stretched over card disc, slashed turnings lapped and glued to the back
(d) Oversewing the two covered discs together with beaded stitches, with fabric loop stitched in place

121 Mother's Day pincushion, with beads and sequins held down by long pins. (*Jane Davies*)

122 Embroidery and beads on fabric to decorate cylindrical houses with beaded or padded lids. Either furnished with a removable doll's house interior, or fitted out as a needlework box. (*Joan Appleton Fisher*)

the oven to remove all moisture. Sew up the seams in both the inner and outer casings.

Use brass lace pins and thread through a sequence of bead and sequin, or small bead, large bead and shaped sequin, to the planned design.

Practical pincushions

The bead embroidery is best confined to the sides and outer edges of this type of pincushion, leaving the central area clear for the pins.

Finishings

Beaded fringes or bead edgings may be applied to either type of pincushion. Traditionally, beaded loops were used to decorate the sides and edges. Do not make the loops too long. They should be placed along the seam line.

Needlecases

The bead embroidery on a needlecase is best worked on a small scale. As the needlecase is often slipped into a workbox, pocket or handbag, the beads should not protrude to catch on anything. Felt

is an ideal material, both for making the needlecase and to allow smaller beads to sink within the fabric. The design can be worked entirely in beads or combined with hand or machine embroidery. Work linear machine stitching first, then add the beading before the needlecase is cut out. Either stretch a large felt piece in a circular embroidery frame, or insert a smaller piece of felt into a calico backing which is then framed.

Apply the beads and bugles so that they follow the linear machine stitching. Add beading after hand embroidery is finished or work at the same time using the method for beaded stitchery.

Construction

Whether the needlecase is square, rectangular or oval, cut the pattern to include a back and front, with a centre fold.

Cut a second piece of felt as a lining the same size as the outer needlecase in a similar or contrasting colour. Pin the two together and finish the edges as one. Either machine with an automatic pattern or straight machine stitch and trim with pinking shears to give a serrated edge. A hand-sewn edge could include beading in the stitchery.

The felt or fabric 'leaves' for holding the needles and pins are cut out with pinking shears. Fold the leaves in half and sew into the centre of the needlecase. Fasten the case with a bead and loop, or a pair of ribbon ties.

Quilted needlecases

Work the beading as an integral part of the quilted design or add beads to already quilted fabric. The backing layer of the quilting forms the lining of the needlecase. Machine all round close to the outer edges, trim off closely and neaten with a bias binding.

Toy houses

A section of cylindrical card tubing or an empty tin forms the base for the little house. The cylinder is covered outside with a rectangle of felt or fabric as wide as the circumference and as tall as the cylinder. Joan Appleton Fisher furnishes the inside with a removable toy house interior, or it can be divided as a receptacle for needlework tools.

Embroider and bead the outer fabric, sew up the back and slip onto the cylinder like a sleeve. Cut a rectangle of thin card, the size of the inner cylinder, cover with fabric, join to form another cylinder and slip inside. Any spacers for needlework tools, made from fabric strips, should be sewn on first. Oversew inner and outer edges together at the top. Cover a circle of card for the base and stitch to the outer cover round the lower edge. Finish with a padded lid that can double as a pincushion.

Beaded book covers

The design area for beading is limited to the front and spine of a book cover as the back of the book needs to lie flat.

The occasion for which the book is intended and the subject content will influence both the design choices and the method of construction. The bead embroidery is always worked before the book cover is cut out.

Constructing a cover

The cover is made with sleeve ends into which the front and back boards fit. The measurements should be taken with a tape measure held to the mid-width point of the inside front board, out across the front, round the spine, across the back and to the inside mid-width point of the back board. Allow 2.5 cm (1 in.) on the two outer edges for turnings.

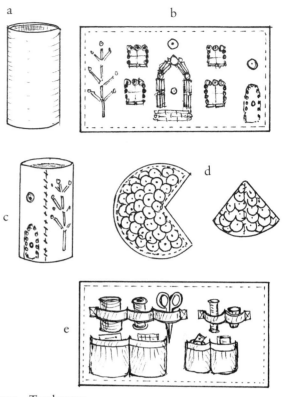

123 Toy houses
(a) Cylinder to be covered
(b) Layout of house embroidery
(c) Fabric oblong joined at the back and slipped onto the cylinder
(d) Conical roof section embroidered with sequins
(e) Arrangement of fabric loops and pockets for needlework tools sewn to the lining before seaming the ends and inserting into the cylinder

Measure the height of the book and allow similar turnings. Cut a lining fabric the same size. Mark the seam allowances onto the fabric with a tacking thread and machine both pieces together along these lines, top and bottom, wrong sides facing outwards. Turn to the right side and press from the lining side. Turn the end seam allowances in and slip stitch them together.

Place the cover over the book and gauge the amount of tension needed to hold the fabric taut when the ends are folded over the front and back boards. Pin in position, remove the book and oversew the top and bottom of each sleeve end.

Finish by sewing a braid, cord or row of beading across both top and bottom edges.

Suitable fabrics

Choose the fabric with care. It should not stretch

124   Beaded book cover. Subject, the Victorian era. Decoration in pearls and pearlized leaves with some embroidery stitches. (*Angela Thompson*)

and should be fairly firm. A closely woven but not too heavy fabric will be easier to handle. It may be advisable to put in an interlining. Domett or a very fine quilting wadding can give a slight roundness to the book. A light iron-on interfacing may be necessary on finer fabrics.

Detached decorations

Attach a separate beaded decoration to a bow of white ribbon around a wedding prayerbook.

Machine-quilted leaves and flower petals are beaded, cut out and then wired. They are sewn together, or held in place with the addition of beads threaded on wire and all secured to the ribbon.

Hanging pockets

An embroidered hanging bag in the author's collection was the inspiration for the hanging pockets in beaded patchwork, designed and made by Joan

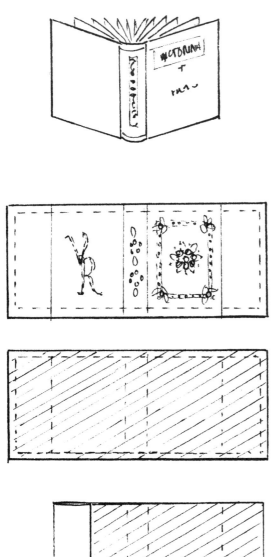

126 Hanging pockets. Detail of one pocket front showing patchwork hexagons outlined with beads, bead oversewn seams and decorative bead loops. (*Joan Appleton Fisher*)

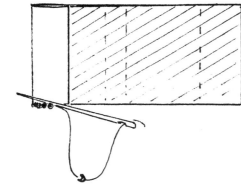

125 Book cover
(a) Book ready to be covered
(b) Seam allowances marked, bead embroidery worked on front and spine, flat embroidery on the back area
(c) Lining cut to the same size
(d) Lining and top sewn together and turned to right side. First end flap turned over to make sleeve pocket for the front book board, sewn with beaded stitchery

Appleton Fisher. The original hand-embroidered bag comes from Madhya Pradesh in Northern India and was used by the nomadic Banjara tribe. It would hang from the tent roof and form a useful receptacle for small articles. Groups of cowrie shells are threaded onto cloth strips and give weight as well as decoration.

The pattern is based on a formation of fabric squares. The central square has an additional square sewn onto each side. When laid out flat, this makes a square cross. When it hangs from the centrally placed cord, the four outside squares, which are double, hang down to form the pockets. The outside of the pockets could be decorated in a variety of ways, making the bag suitable for children or for adult use.

Joan Appleton Fisher has applied hexagons in graded layers on each outside pocket and bordered them with tiny beads. The centre square is divided into the central hanging area with four border panels, with a fabric-covered beaded button to hold the pocket fastening loops.

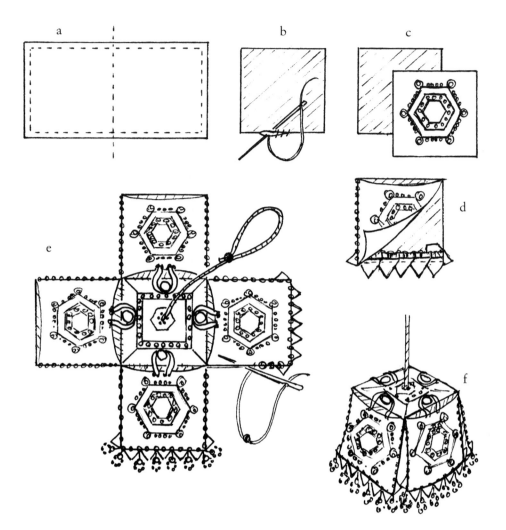

127 Hanging pockets

(a) Fabric piece, 36 cm by 18 cm (14 in. by 7 in.) with seam allowances added. Cut 9

(b) Piece folded in half and seamed up the sides. Turned to right side and slip stitched together on bottom seam

(c) Pocket pair, plain back and a decorated front

(d) Pocket pair oversewn with beads on the side seams, mitred strip triangles inserted into hem, tacked, then sewn with beads

(e) Pocket pairs assembled into a cross. Central portion with hanging cord and buttons for the pocket loops

(f) Finished hanging pocket

The outer squares are edged with folded triangles. A tiny beaded loop hangs between each triangle and onto the corners. The lower hem and side edges are decorated with tiny beads, alternating red and yellow, sewn with gold Lurex thread.

Construction

Draw out a rectangle on pattern paper 36 cm (14 in.) long by 18 cm (7 in.) wide. Add seam allowance. Cut nine fabric pieces and mark the seam lines.

Take eight fabric pieces and fold each one in half, right sides together to make 18-cm (7-in.) squares. Tack and machine along the seam line on the three sides of each square, leaving an opening of approximately 5 m (2 in.). This is for turning the square through to the right side. Press the turned square and slip stitch the opening together neatly.

Apply patchwork or beaded decoration to one side of four of these squares, having the fold at the top.

Central square

Machine together the two outside seams but leave the bottom open. Turn to the right side and press the lower seam allowances under. Mark the centre

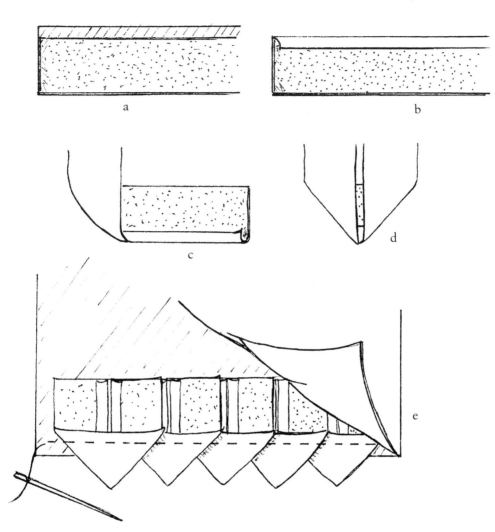

128 Method for making a triangular border from mitred strips
(a) Cut iron-on interfacing narrower than the fabric strip. Iron on, keeping lower edges level
(b) Turn the seam allowance over and iron in place
(c) Fold up the first mitre
(d) Fold up the second mitre to make a point, seam-turning to the middle
(e) Turn to straight side and cut from the strip, leaving 2.5 cm (1 in.) extra both sides. Lay in position and tack firmly

of this top fabric square by tacking across both the diagonals from corner to corner, top layer only. To give firmness to this top hanging area, cut a piece of thick card, approximately 10 cm (4 in.) square. Pierce a hole exactly in the centre of the card with a metal skewer.

Insert the card between the fabric layers and match the central card hole with the centre tacking thread and keep the top and sides parallel to the fabric square. With a matching thread, tack through both layers of fabric, keeping close to the card edges to hold it in position. This tacking line may be covered with beading or chain stitching afterwards.

Cut strips of patterned fabric 2.5 cm (1 in.) in width plus seam allowances. Apply these as a border to the top of the fabric square surrounding the stiffened card centre. Mitre the corners and sew tiny beads round both the inner square and the outside of the fabric border.

Assembling the finished squares
Place one of the four bead-embroidered squares on top of each plain square with the folded edges at the top. Oversew the side edges of each set of squares together, taking a bead with every stitch. A metallic sewing thread will give a decorative effect to the stitchery. A patchwork border is inserted between the unsewn bottom edges.

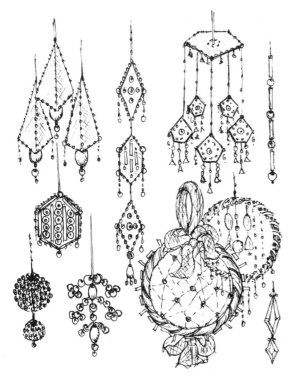

129 Ideas for beaded baubles. Triangular bells, hexagon pendants, pentagon mobile, beaded balls, strung beads and covered, beaded rings.

Folded patchwork border

Cut patterned fabric strips 4 cm (1¼ in.) wide. Cut iron-on interfacing approximately 0.5cm (¼ in.) narrower and iron onto the wrong side of the fabric. Press the narrow seam allowance over the interfacing onto the wrong side. These strips are folded at right-angles so that the pressed edge forms a mitre. Cut off the mitred strip, leaving enough seam allowance to be hidden when the triangle is inserted between the bottom layers of the pockets. Stitch all together on the edges and decorate with beads.

Attach the four completed pockets, decorated side uppermost, to the central square by oversewing together along each inner top edge, leaving the pocket tops open.

Fastenings

Sew bead-decorated, fabric-covered buttons onto the middle of each border strip on the central panel. Make a fabric rouleau loop and sew to the top of each pocket. Decorate the loop base with a row of tiny beads. Thread a cord up through the central hole of the reinforcing card and out to the top, holding beneath with a knot. Tie a loop in the other end to hang the pockets from.

Anniversary and Christmas cards

Choose a design that reflects the occasion: the name or initial letter of the recipient, a favourite flower or colour, wedding bells or the date of an anniversary. Special-occasion cards, for example for a silver or golden wedding, should be worked in the appropriate colours. Christmas card designs may include lettering, beaded holly, a tree with bead decorations, the Star of Bethlehem. Whichever you choose, keep the work area small and simplify the design. Allow enough fabric for placing into the card mount. Purchased mounts are available with rectangular, round or oval cut-outs and ready-stick backing. Cut a piece of thin quilting wadding the size of the cut-out and place beneath the embroidery, which is trimmed to at least 1.5 cm (½ in.) bigger than the cut-out. Place the wadding down first, then the beaded fabric and press the adhesive card backings together.

If the card has no adhesive backing, hold the fabric in place with double-sided sticky tape. This is safer than using fabric adhesive.

Frames and paperweights

More elaborate designs can be mounted in a small gilt frame or placed beneath a hollowed, domed paperweight. The construction method in both cases is the same as for the bead pendant: the seam allowance is slit, folded and glued over a backing card. Glue a second piece of card behind to cover the raw edges. Bulky fabrics can be backed with double-sided interfacing. This obviates the necessity for turnings. The paperweight is held down with a minimum of fabric adhesive round the outer rim.

Beaded baubles for a Christmas tree and other decorations

Beaded rings

First cover the ring by binding with ribbon or decorative fabric strips. Beads are sewn onto the bound circle afterwards, or separate bead strings are wound on top of the fabric. Criss-cross the circle centre with glitter threads or free machine-embroidered lines and add more beads afterwards. Hang drop fringes and pendant beads within the circle and from the lower edge.

Patchwork shapes

Three-dimensional geometric shapes are covered

130 Beaded box lid with ribbon border sewn with beads, and bead quilted interior. (*Margaret Jackson, City and Guilds Embroidery*)

and seamed together with beads. Cut out thick card templates, a piece for each pattern section. Cover each with glitter fabric by glueing the seam allowances to the back with fabric adhesive. Alternatively, use double-sided interfacing. Oversew shapes together with a bead to each stitch. Add drop beads and sequins.

Three long triangles are sewn to form a bell. Two hexagon shapes are covered and seamed together flat. Small pentagons hang from the points of a larger pentagon as a beaded mobile. To finish, add loops for hanging made of beaded thread.

Boxes and box lids

Both the lid and sides of the box provide areas for bead application, with or without quilting. Trapunto quilting with the addition of beads works well as any irregularity of fabric tension caused by the beadwork can be taken up by the quilting.

The eventual use of the box should be taken into consideration when planning the position of the

beadwork and a suitable and functional fastening should be devised. This might be in the form of a beaded cord or tassel. A beaded, quilted lining will help unite the assembled design.

For further information, consult *Embroidered Boxes* by Jane Lemon.

Lampshades

Plan any bead designs as if they are to be worked on transparent fabric. Construction methods should not show when the light is on. Bead edgings or fringes can be sewn to the shade *in situ*, or first sewn to a braid which is applied afterwards. Use any of the bead looping or fringing methods described in Chapter 8.

Fabric for a cylindrical lamp base is first embroidered and then seamed up one side and pulled over a card tube like a sleeve. Choose a very simple design if the shade and lamp base are to be worked as a pair.

131 Circular box and lid. Hand embroidery stitches, including woven wheels, combined with beads. (*Helen Archibald*)

Toys

Toys and patchwork balls are embroidered before the pattern pieces are cut out. Any machine embroidery is worked first, before the beading. Remember to leave the seam allowances clear. Some beads may be added afterwards to complete the design.

Many other articles are of course suitable for the inclusion of beadwork.

132 Toy elephant with beaded eyelashes. Beads added to straight stitch free machine embroidery on felt. Adaptation of a commercial pattern. (*Angela Thompson*)

Glossary

AGGREY BEADS Trade beads from West Africa

AMULET Object worn against evil

APPLIQUE One fabric which is applied by stitchery to another

AUTOMATIC STITCH Decorative stitch controlled from within the sewing machine

AWL Sharp-pointed tool for piercing holes

BARTER BEADS Beads used as currency

BEAD Small, round object, pierced for threading or ornamentation

BEADING NEEDLE Long, thin needle with a round eye

BERLIN WOOLWORK Nineteenth-century canvas embroidery in wools

BOG OAK Substitute for jet

BOW-DRILL Drill attached to the thong of a bow

BOW-LOOM Primitive loom with the warp thread tensioned with a curved bow

BUGLE Narrow tubular bead

CANVAS WORK Counted-thread embroidery worked onto evenweave, stiffened fabric

CHARLOTTE Faceted round bead

CHENILLE NEEDLE Sharp-pointed needle with a large, oval eye

CHECK PURL Square-section tubular metal thread

CHINTZ Flower-patterned fabric of Eastern origin popular in the late eighteenth century

CORNELY MACHINE Industrial chain-stitch machine

COUCHING Embroidery stitch used to hold down a second thread

COUVETTE Cup-shaped sequin

COWRIE Marine shell found in the Indian Ocean

DIAMANTÉ Imitation diamond beads usually sold on adhesive strips of iron-on backing

DISSOLVABLE FABRIC Spun-alginate fabric which dissolves in boiling water used for lace-textured embroidery

DRAW-BACK STITCH Tambour embroidery stitch

DRAWN THREAD WORK Embroidery on evenweave fabric with some warp and weft threads removed

DROP Bead which hangs like a pendant

EMBROIDERY STONES Glass or semiprecious stones with drilled holes

EYE BEADS Glass beads with spots to depict eyes often used as cult objects

FAIENCE Early form of glass made from quartz and lime

FEED TEETH Device on the machine bed to control stitch length and move the fabric beneath the needle

FREE MACHINE EMBROIDERY Embroidery worked in a circular frame with the machine foot removed and feed teeth out of action

FRENCH JET Imitation jet made from black glass

GRISAILLE Victorian beadwork in shades of grey and white

HEDEBO Type of Danish embroidery which features buttonholed rings

ICON Religious image in the form of a picture or statue

IMAGE ROBE Embroidered garment to clothe image statues in Catholic churches

ITALIAN QUILTING Parallel channels sewn onto double fabric with a thick yarn threaded into the back

JET Form of sea coal

JEWELLERY BEADS Gold or silver metal beads

JEWELLERY FINDINGS Small metal parts which separate necklace beads

JEWELLERY STONES Claw-set semiprecious stones

KNITTING BEADS Round beads with yarn-sized holes

LAMPBEAD Handmade bead made by the winding process

LAZY SQUAW STITCH, LAZY STITCH Short strings of beads sewn into the ground cloth at intervals

MARGUERITE Daisy-shaped crystal bead

MARVER The process of flattening a bead into a cylinder

METAL THREAD Gold and silver thread used in embroidery

MICA Talc crystals first used in shisha work

MILLEFIORI Glass process with patterns obtained from sliced glass rods

MIRROR WORK Another name for shisha work

MITRED CORNER Seam joined at an angle to reduce excess fabric

MOSS STITCH Loopy stitch worked on the Cornely machine

NEEDLEPOINT LACE Needle-stitched lace

NEEDLEWEAVING Embroidery on evenweave fabric with threads withdrawn one way

OPUS ANGLICANUM English ecclesiastical embroidery of the late thirteenth to early fourteenth century

OVERLAID STITCH Couching stitch to hold strings of beads

PAILLETTE Original name for sequin

PAILLETTE PERCE Shaped paillete

PAPILLON Stamped fancy metallic shape, sometimes coloured

PASSEMENTERIE Trimming decorated with beads and sequins

PENDANT BEAD One which hangs with a hole pierced horizontally through the top

PENELOPE CANVAS Double-thread canvas

PORCUPINE EMBROIDERY Another name for quill work

POUND BEADS Even-shaped round beads for Berlin woolwork sold by the pound

PRESSED BEADS Beads made in a mould

PURL Tubular metal thread formed like a wound spring

QUILL WORK North American Indian embroidery using flattened, dyed porcupine quills

REED Gathered fold in the construction of smocking

REGALIA Ceremonial costume and accoutrements

RING FRAME Circular embroidery frame with inner and outer rings

ROCAILLE Smooth, round bead

RONDEL Faceted crystal bead

ROSETTE Flower-shaped crystal bead

ROULEAU Narrow, tubular strips made from bias fabric

SABLÉ Fine beads, closely laid, eighteenth century

SEED BEAD Small, round bead

SEQUIN Stamped metal or plastic shape with central hole, or holes on the circumference

SHISHA WORK Small pieces of mirror or mica applied with a network of buttonhole stitches

SLATE FRAME Rectangular frame with adjustable sides enabling fabric to be kept at tension

SPANGLE Flat, round sequin with a hole in the middle

STUMPWORK Raised Stuart embroidery, incorporating needlepoint stitches

TAILOR-TACKING FOOT Machine foot with a central flange which forms looped stitches

TAMBOUR HOOK Handle with separate hooked needles for chain stitching

TAMBOUR FRAME Circular frame for working tambour embroidery

TAMBOUR STITCH Chain stitch worked with the tambour hook

TAPESTRY NEEDLE Blunt-pointed needle with an elongated eye

TEMPLATE Pattern shape which is drawn round

TOSCA Round bead with square-cut hole

TRADE BEADS Beads used as barter

TRAPUNTO QUILTING Double fabric padded in certain stitched areas by introducing stuffing from behind

TUBE BEAD Long cylindrical bead or bugle

TUBE Another name for smocking reeds

UTILITY STITCHES Sewing-machine stitches for neatening hems and edges

VESTMENTS Garments worn in a religious connection by the clergy

WADDED QUILTING Top fabric, wadding and lining, stitched through all three layers

WADDING Padding inserted into quilting

WAMPUM North American Indian shell beads made from the *quahog* clam

WARP Longitudinal threads in weaving construction

WEFT Lateral threads in weaving construction

WHIPPED STITCH Free sewing-machine stitch worked with a tight top and loose bottom tension

WOUND BEADS Made by winding molten glass round a metal rod

Bibliography

Beads, historical

CLABBURN, Pamela, *Beadwork*, Shire Publications, 1980.
EDWARDS, Joan, *Bead Embroidery*, Batsford, 1966.
GILL, Anne E., *Beadwork - The Technique of Stringing, Threading and Weaving*, Batsford, 1976.
HINKS, Peter, *Jewellery*, Hamlyn All-colour Paperbacks, Paul Hamlyn, 1969.
LAYE, H.E., *Batsford Encyclopaedia of Crafts*, Batsford, 1978.
MOOI, Hetty, *The Bead Book*, Ida-Merete Erlando and Van Nostrand Reinhold, New York, 1974.
MOWAT ERIKSON, Joan, *The Universal Bead*, W. W. Norton and Co., New York, 1969.
MULLER, Helen, *Jet Jewellery and Ornaments*, Shire Publications, 1980.
SEYD, Mary, *Introducing Beads*, Batsford, 1973.
STRADAL, Marianne, *Needlecraft with Beads and Crystals*, Mills and Boon, 1971.
WHITE, Mary, *How to do Beadwork*, Dover Publications, 1972 (first published 1904 by Doubleday, Page and Co.).

Beads, ethnic

CAMPBELL, Margaret, *From the Hands of the Hills*, Copyright Media Transasia, published by J.S. Uberoi, Hong Kong, 1978.
CAREY, Margaret, *Beads and Beadwork of East and South Africa*, Shire Publications, 1986.
CRILL, Rosemary, *Hats from India*, Exhibition Catalogue, Victoria and Albert Museum, 1985.
DOCKSTRADER, Frederick J., *Weaving Arts of the North American Indian*, James J. Kery Ltd, 1978.
FAGG, William, *Yoruba Beadwork, Art of Nigeria*, Rizzoli International Publications Inc., New York, 1980.
GOSTELOW, Mary, *Embroidery, Traditional Designs, Techniques and Patterns from all over the World*, Marshall Cavendish Editions, 1977.

MORRIS, Jean, and LEVITAS, Ben, *South African Tribal Life Today*, College Press, Cape Town, 1984.
NATIONAL GALLERY OF ART, WASHINGTON, U.S.A., Exhibition Catalogue, *Ancient Art of the American Woodland Indians*, published by the Board of Trustees, National Gallery of Art, 1985.
PEARLSTONE MATHEWS, Zena, *Color and Shape in American Indian Art*, The Metropolitan Museum of Art, New York, 1983.
YACOPINO, Feliccia, *Threadlines Pakistan*, The Ministry of Industries, Government of Pakistan, 1977.

Beads in fashion

BANBURY, Gisela, and DEWAR, Angela, *Embroidery for Fashion*, Batsford, 1985.
BOWMAN, Sara, *A Fashion for Extravagance: Art Deco Fabrics and Fashions*, Bell & Hyman, 1985.
CONTINI, Mila, *Fashion from Ancient Egypt to the Present Day*, Paul Hamlyn, 1965.
FOSTER, Vanda, *Bags and Purses*, Batsford, 1982.

Historical bead embroidery

EDWARDS, Joan, *Berlin Work*, Joan Edwards' Small Books, Bayford Books, 1980.
FISHER, Joan, *The Creative Art of Needlepoint Tapestry*, Hamlyn, 1972.
KENDRICK, A. F., *English Needlework*, A. & C. Black Ltd, 1933.
PROCTOR, Molly G., *Victorian Canvas Work: Berlin Wool Work*, Batsford, 1972, paperback 1986.
SNOOK, Barbara, *English Embroidery*, Mills & Boon, 1974.
SYNGE, Lanto, *Antique Needlework*, Blandford Press, 1982.

Stitches and embroidery techniques

BUTLER, Anne, *Batsford Encyclopaedia of Embroidery Stitches*, Batsford, 1979, paperback 1983.
DAWSON, Barbara, *Technique of Metal Thread Embroidery*, Batsford, 1968 and 1976, paperback 1985.
EMBROIDERERS' GUILD, PRACTICAL STUDY GROUP, *Needlework School*, Windward, 1984.
HOWARD, Constance, *The Constance Howard Book of Stitches*, Batsford, 1979, paperback 1985.
JOHN, Edith, *Needleweaving*, Batsford, 1970, paperback 1987
LEMON, Jane, *Embroidered Boxes*, Batsford, 1984, paperback, 1986.
LOVESEY, Nenia, *Needlepoint Lace*, Batsford, 1980.
RHODES, Mary, *Batsford Book of Canvas Work*, Batsford, 1983.
SWIFT, Gay, *The Batsford Encylopaedia of Embroidery Techniques*, Batsford, 1984.

Machine embroidery

COLEMAN, Anne, *The Creative Sewing Machine*, Batsford, 1979.
MCNEILL, Moyra, *Machine Embroidery: Lace and See-Through Techniques*, Batsford, 1985.
RISLEY, Christine, *Machine Embroidery, A Complete Guide*, Studio Vista, 1973.
THOMPSON, Angela, *Machine Embroidery*, paperback, Macdonald Educational Ltd, 1979 and W. I. Books, 1979.
THOMPSON, Angela, *The Complete Book of the Sewing Machine*, Paul Hamlyn, 1980 and paperback, W. I. Books, 1980.

Smocking

HALL, Maggie, *Smocks*, Shire Publications, 1979.
KEAY, Diana, *Smocking*, Needle Crafts No. 5, Search Press, 1979.
KEAY, Diana, *New Ideas for Smocking*, Leaflet, The Embroiderers' Guild, 1983.
PYMAN, Kit (Ed.), *Every Kind of Smocking*, Search Press, 1985.
THOM, Margaret, *Smocking in Embroidery*, Batsford, 1972.

Quilting

AVERY, Virginia, *Quilts to Wear*, Bell & Hyman, 1982.
COLBY, Averil, *Quilting*, Batsford, 1972.
SHORT, Eirian, *Introducing Quilting*, Batsford, 1974.

Tambour beading

EDWARDS, Joan, *The Bead Embroidered Dress*, Joan Edwards, Small Books, Bayford Books, 1985.
JOHNSON, Beryl, *Advanced Embroidery Techniques*, Batsford, 1983.

Beads and sequins

CAMPBELL-HARDING, Valerie, *Textures in Embroidery*, Batsford, 1977, Paperback 1985.
MESSENT, Jan, *Embroidery and Nature*, Batsford, 1980, paperback 1983.
—*Embroidery and Animals*, Batsford, 1984.
—*Embroidery and Architecture*, Batsford, 1985.

Places to visit where beads and beadwork may be found

Beaver House, London EC4 (Hudson's Bay Company Headquarters)
British Museum, London WC1
Horniman Museum, Forest Hill, London SE23
Museum of Mankind, Burlington Gardens, London W1
Victoria and Albert Museum, South Kensington, London SW7

Ashmolean Museum, Oxford
Birmingham City Museum and Art Gallery
Embroiderers' Guild Collection, Apartment 41, Hampton Court Palace, Surrey
Ethnographical Museum, Cambridge (Beck Collection)
Museum of Costume and Textiles, Castlegate, Nottingham

A selection of Museums to visit abroad

The Metropolitan Museum, New York
Smithsonian Institute, Washington
The Gold Museum, Bogota, Colombia
The Archaeological Museum, Lima, Peru
The Archaeological Museum, Athens
Heraklion Museum, Crete

Many other museums and institutions have collections of beads or beadwork. It is always worth enquiring if you are in the area.

Suppliers

Beads and sequins

Bead Shop
43 Neal Street, London WC2H 9PJ

Creative Beadcraft Ltd
Unit 26, Chiltern Trading Estate, Earl Howe Road, Holmer Green, High Wycombe, Buckinghamshire

Ells and Farrier Ltd
5 Princes Street, Hanover Square, London W1

Janet Coles Beads
Perdiswell Cottage, Bilford Road, Worcester WR3 8QA

Kaleidoscope
3 Grove Park, Brislington, Bristol BS4 3LG

Necklace Maker Workshop
25 Portobello Green, London W10 5TZ

Offshoot Woodville Craft Centre
Burton Road, Woodville, Nr Burton-on-Trent DE11 7JW

Straight Lines (UK) Ltd
1 Straight Lines House, New Road, Newtown, Powys SY16 1BB

Beads and knitting beads

Metropolitan Sewing Machines
321 Ashley Road, Parkstone, Poole, Dorset BH4 0AP

Wykraft Products
Mail Order Department, 8 Tarrant Way, Moulton, Northampton NN3 1UF

Many craft shops and department stores have a selection of beads and sequins.

Fabrics

Mawata silk wadding

Sue Harris
The Mill, Tregoyd Mill, Three Cocks, Brècon,
Powys LD3 0SW

Spun alginate (hot-water-dissolvable fabric),
muslins and linings, polyester wadding, silks
cottons, synthetics:

McCulloch and Wallace
25-26 Dering Street, London W1

Whaleys (Bradford) Ltd
Harris Court, Great Horton, Bradford, West
Yorkshire BD7 4EQ

Gemstones and crystals

Goldilocks Components
Perwick Bay, Port St. Mary, Isle of Man

Lapidary Shop
26 Waterloo Road, Burslem, Stoke-on-Trent, Staffs
ST6 3ES

Manchester Minerals
Rooth Street, Heaton Norris, Stockport, Cheshire
SK4 IDJ

The Stone Corner
42a High Street, Hastings, East Sussex TN4 3ES

Threads

de Denne Ltd
159/161 Kenton Road, Kenton, Harrow,
Middlesex

Mace and Nairn
86 Crane Street, Salisbury, Wiltshire

A variety of fabrics and threads is also available
from craft shops and department stores.

Bead suppliers in the USA

Bead Different
7 West Quincy, Westmont, Illinois 60559

International Importing Bead and Novelty Co. Inc
17 North State Street, Chicago, Illinois 60602

Larraways
Balboa Island, California 92662

The Bead Shop
812 South Coast Highway, Laguana Beach,
California 92651

The Freed Company
415 Central N.W., Box 394, Albuquerque, NM
87103

Index